Hong Kong

by

JUDY BONAVIA

Judy Bonavia was born in Perth, Western Australia and has
lived in the Far East since 1962. She writes travel articles and
specialises in China's culture and minority peoples. She has
written guidebooks on the Silk Road and the Yangtse River.
She lived in China for a number of years and speaks and
reads Mandarin. Judy Bonavia lives in Hong Kong.

AA

Produced by the Publishing Division of
The Automobile Association

Written by Judy Bonavia
Peace and Quiet section by Paul
Sterry
Consultant: Frank Dawes

Edited, designed and produced by
the Publishing Division of The
Automobile Association. Maps ©
The Automobile Association 1990

Distributed in the United Kingdom
by the Publishing Division of The
Automobile Association, Fanum
House, Basingstoke, Hampshire,
RG21 2EA

A CIP catalogue record for this book
is available from the British Library.

ISBN 0 86145 871-0

Published by The Automobile
Association

Typesetting: Tradespools Ltd, Frome,
Somerset
Colour separation: L C Repro,
Aldermaston
Printing: Printers S. R. L., Trento, Italy

Front cover picture: Chinese junk

INTRODUCTION	4
BACKGROUND	6
HONG KONG ISLAND	12-36
KOWLOON	37-44
NEW TERRITORIES	45-56
OUTLYING ISLANDS	57-60
PEACE AND QUIET: Wildlife and Countryside in Hong Kong	61-72
FOOD AND DRINK	73
SHOPPING	87
ACCOMMODATION	93
NIGHTLIFE AND ENTERTAINMENT	98
WEATHER AND WHEN TO GO	101
HOW TO BE A LOCAL	103
SPECIAL EVENTS	104
CHILDREN	108
TIGHT BUDGET	109
SPORTING ACTIVITIES	109
DIRECTORY	111-124
LANGUAGE	125
INDEX	127

This book employs a
simple rating system to
help choose which places
to visit:

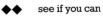 ◆◆◆   do not miss

◆◆   see if you can

◆   worth seeing if
you have time

Hong Kong, the 'barren island' of the 19th century, is now thriving, busy and crowded

INTRODUCTION

Hong Kong entices from the first moment of arrival, plunging the visitor into an exhilarating miniature world of ancient Chinese tradition and 20th-century Mammonism.

These work together harmoniously: the pin-striped suited Hong Kong businessman, communicating with the financial capitals of the world from his 30th floor office, may consult a fortune teller on each important transaction. Buddhist monks exorcise a run of bad luck from the grounds of one of the most modern race-tracks in the world. A geomancer calculates the exact hour at which the Hong Kong & Shanghai Bank's bronze lion statues may be safely moved. The contrasts are endless: elegant boutiques and shopping arcades compete with makeshift

stalls and market alleys; skyscrapers peer down
on old temple roofs; expensive restaurants
disregard the food stalls on the nearby
pavement, and residents of luxurious apartment
buildings have little in common with shanty town
dwellers and housing estate occupants.
Change is at the heart of this city-state. The
ability to determine market forces and adjust
rapidly to them applies as much to the street
hawker with his barrow as to the manufacturing
magnate on his factory floor.
The racy pace is set by Hong Kong people,
eager to get a good job or open a successful
business, provide for their families and, above
all, give their children as good an education as
possible. In the typical Cantonese dream, the
native son will go abroad and build a successful
career, sending back money to his relatives and

eventually enabling them to join him permanently, away from the pressures and insecurity about the future which give Hong Kong life its edge.

Added to it all is the sheer beauty of the harbour, the stunning vistas and the tranquillity of its hillsides.

BACKGROUND

The discovery of pottery sherds, stone tools and iron implements in various parts of Hong Kong attests to an early occupation of the area. The natural riches of its land and sea encouraged agriculture and fishing, but its sheltered bays were the haunts of pirates. Harassment of settled communities and coastal trade became so intense during the Ch'ing Dynasty (221BC–206BC) that the Emperor ordered all inhabitants to withdraw from the area, creating a 'free fire' zone to eradicate the pirates. It took decades before the communities returned.

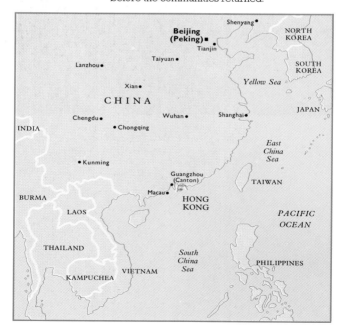

Crowds of worshippers come to make offerings of food at Kowloon's modern Wong Tai Sin Temple, built in traditional Chinese style

For many years, China cherished a unique and separate identity; Europeans did not begin to arrive until the 16th century. Even then, for more than a century the Chinese court was able to contain increasing European demands for access to the rich markets of China by confining their activities to the minute Portuguese colony of Macau. But by the 18th century 'factories' (warehouses) had been established at Canton from which foreign companies traded in China's silk, tea and porcelain, which were much in demand in America and Europe.

As the Indian opium trade, dominated by the British, Portuguese and Americans, began to drain the silver coffers of China, the imperial court became ever more alarmed at the deleterious effect of 'foreign mud' on its people and economy. Meanwhile, Britain clamoured for wider access to Chinese markets and was prepared to back its demands with impressive naval might. The Viceroy of Canton, Lin Tse-hsu, took the provocative step of burning the foreigners' chests of opium, setting the stage for the Opium Wars (1839–42 and 1856–60). A British fleet which sailed up the China coast and along the Yangtse River met with brave but ineffective resistance, and was able to impose the 1842 Treaty of Nanjing upon the humiliated Manchu Ch'ing court. This unequal treaty demanded a huge indemnity from the Chinese, the opening of treaty ports, and the cession to Britain of the island of Hong Kong. The convention of Peking in 1860 ceded Kowloon Peninsula and in 1898 the New Territories' 99-year lease was signed.

Hong Kong thrived, in spite of the malaria which killed off many a European in the first decades of the colony. It had become an important port for merchant and passenger ships along the southeast Asian trade route, a centre for careening and refitting vessels, and by the end of the century had an annual trade turnover of £50 million. Opium continued to be a major source of income, and the Hong Kong government's monopoly on opium processing in the colony continued until the late 1930s.

Its population was to swell with each successive upheaval in China and by the eve of the Japanese invasion in World War II numbered over 1.6 million. Hong Kong fell on Christmas Day, 1941. Many Chinese fled back to the mainland; others were deported. With the re-establishment of the British administration in 1946, the population increased by 100,000 a month, to be swelled yet again by China's civil war. The fall of Shanghai to the Communists in 1949–50 was to bring about Hong Kong's transition into a major manufacturing centre. Shanghai businessmen arrived with their textile, banking and business expertise, and their capital, and founded flourishing enterprises.

In 1984 the joint Sino-British declaration on the return of Hong Kong to mainland China in 1997 was initialled. This set the scene for long-term negotiations on the government which will represent the territory over the next 50 years as a Special Administrative Region of China.

Hong Kong's 414 square miles (1,071 sq km) supports a population of around 5.7 million. It is totally dependent on daily food supplies from mainland China.

Hong Kong's rich inheritance of culture and tradition is always apparent. This bridegroom's costume dates back to the Sung dynasty

Away from the dense crowds of Hong Kong Island, the core of the colony, are areas still uninhabited by man. Hong Kong consists of 236 islands altogether, as well as parts of the mainland bordering China: the Kowloon peninsula and, beyond, the New Territories, which also take in the 235 outlying islands. The diversity of these areas is what makes Hong Kong so special; a visit there is an unforgettable experience.

HONG KONG

—— Mass Transit Railway

CHINA

Hau Hoi Wan
(Deep Bay)

Sham Chun River

Lo Wu

Lok Ma Chau Lookout

Sheung Shui

Mai Po • San Tin

Tin Shui Wan

Lau Fau Shan •

Ngau Tam Mei

Ping Shan

Yuen Long

Kat Hing Wai Walled Village • Pat Heung

Ha Tsuen •

Kam Tin • Shek Kong

Ching Chung Koon Temple

New Territories

Black Point

Lung Kwu Tan

Tuen Mun 583m

Tai Lam Chung Reservoir

Tai Mo Shan ▲ 957m

Castle Peak

Sam Tung UK Museum

Urmston Road

Lung Kwu Chau

Pillar Point

Castle Peak Bay Pearl Island

Tai Lam Chung • Sham Tseng

Tsuen Wan

Ma Wan

Tsing Yi

Kwai Chung

Kap Shui Mun

Tree Island

Sha Chau

Mo To Chau (The Brothers)

Chek Lap Kok

Lantau Island

Discovery Bay

Peng Chau

Kennedy Town

Tung Chung • Fort

Tin Hau Temple Trappist Monastery

Ngong Ping

Po Lin Monastery

Mui Wo

Silver Mine Bay

Tea Gardens

▲ *Lantau Peak* 934m

Tai O •

Pui O

Shek Pik Reservoir

Cheung Sha

Chi Ma Chan Peninsula

Yung Shue Wan

Peaked Hill

Fan Lau Fort

Pak Tai Temple

Cheung Chau

Po Tsai Cave

Lamma Island

▲ 353m

Siu A Chau

Shek Kwu Chau

West Lamma Channel

Lantau Channel

Tai A Chau

Soko Islands

South China Sea

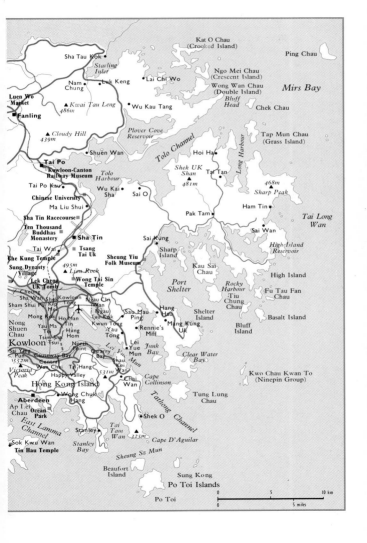

HONG KONG ISLAND

It seems scarcely possible that Lord Palmerston's phrase 'a barren island with hardly a house upon it', uttered in 1841, could actually ever have referred to Hong Kong Island, now one of the most densely populated islands in the world for its size — 1.2 million within 30 square miles (78 sq km). In spite of these astonishing statistics, it is possible to walk for hours through the island's hills where, at every turn, a magnificent view appears and peace and quiet reigns.
The population is sandwiched below the island's steep peaks, crammed along the coast, and creeping up the hillsides in high rise apartment blocks which lean and sway during strong

typhoon winds. For the tourist, the best way to imbibe the contrasting sights of the island is on foot—bemusedly through the expensive shopping complexes of Central District, carefully down the steep narrow market streets of Western, or casually around the Peak with time to absorb the harbour vistas.

Central District and Victoria Peak

CENTRAL DISTRICT

The Central District is the heart of the territory's business and banking world; its tower blocks ram the skyline and crowds jostle and swarm along the pavements. Air conditioned shops, boutiques and shopping arcades proliferate. The construction boom in the territory is nowhere more apparent than in Central, where giant office and shopping complexes are constantly under construction. Among the more spectacular is **The Landmark**, a multi-storey complex of chic shops surrounding a central atrium and fountain where exhibitions and lunchtime concerts are held. The 52-storey **Jardine House**, with its rows of porthole windows, has featured in the TV dramatisation of James Clavell's *Taipan*. Dominating the waterfront, the three towers of **Exchange Square** are most pleasing architecturally, and they house Hong Kong's Stock Exchange, as well as many major international trading companies and merchant banks. Beside the City Hall is another waterfront monument, the distinctive 28-storey Prince of Wales Building in **HMS Tamar**, the Royal Naval Base, with its narrow, pointed base.

In the 1840s the district of Victoria (now Central) was perceived as a European preserve with Chinese areas to the east and west. This pattern appears to have been followed for the first decades more out of tradition than outright racism. Three parallel streets dissect the area—Queen's Road, Des Voeux

Road and Connaught Road. The great business houses of Jardine, Matheson & Co, Butterfield & Swire, John Dent & Co, who dominated the China trade in tea, opium and textiles in the early days of the territory, built their trading headquarters along **Queen's Road Central** which, until the late 1860s, abutted the waterfront. Their company jetties and piers commanded the sampan-cluttered waterfront, and just below the intersection of Queen's Road and Pedder Street stood a public wharf.

Des Voeux Road—named after Sir William Des Voeux, Governor of the Colony from 1887 to 1891—was constructed on reclaimed land in the 1860s and became the heart of Hong Kong's commercial district, with the island's first City Hall being opened by the Duke of Edinburgh, Prince Alfred, in 1869; soon the Hong Kong & Shanghai Bank and the Bank of Canton followed suit, establishing their headquarters in the 1880s. In 1927 Hong Kong Land Co Ltd purchased the Prince's Building site for £3 million, a princely sum in those days, when edifices in Bombay Gothic and arcaded colonial styles were popular. Further reclamation along the harbour front led to the opening of the **Connaught Road** in 1887. During the 1920s the scent of flowers pervaded Wyndham Street, also known as the **Street of Flowers**. Later the flower vendors were moved to **D'Aguilar Street**, where they remain today. The first English language newspaper, the *China Mail*, began publishing on

Wyndham Street in 1845 and so it also gained the nickname 'Fleet Street in miniature'.

At the top of Duddell Street a flight of granite steps leading to Ice House Street has been designated a historical monument and dates from the late 1870s. Four old gas street lamps adorn the flight and create a charming glimpse of old Hong Kong. **Ice House Street** was thus named after an American entrepreneur began shipping lake ice from America by sailing-ship, and storing it here. On the corner of Ice House Street and Lower Albert Road stands a handsome red brick building built in 1904 as an ice house by one of the early Hong Kong companies, Dairy Farm. The building is now occupied by the Foreign Correspondents' Club and is treasured by its members. The Dairy Farm Company introduced a dairy herd to the colony in the 1880s, and it was said that 'nothing brought Hong Kong greater fame among neighbouring colonies and settlements where Europeans were gathered together in the East than the option thus afforded to her favoured residents of dispensing with tinned milk in their cup of tea.'

In 1911 Chinese fashion underwent an abrupt change, bringing another western influence to the fore. The streets of Hong Kong thronged with Chinese gentlemen wearing western clothes and foreign hats as they cut off their long hair as a symbol of solidarity at the overthrow of Manchu rule. Long gowns continued to be favoured

Flower-sellers were once based in Wyndham Street; now their wares sweeten the air in D'Aguilar Street

by the less western-orientated Chinese men, especially the intellectuals. In the 1960s the graceful *cheongsam* was still worn by Chinese women of all ages, but, unfortunately, it has since gone out of fashion.

Walking in Central
A walk westwards along Queen's Road Central reveals the more interesting but less opulent life of Central District. Opposite Lane Crawford's Department Store (an old Hong Kong company which began as a ship's chandler) are two narrow, crowded shopping alleys (Li Yuen Street West and Li Yuen Street East) whose stalls

and shops sell handbags, belts, fabrics and a wide selection of clothing at attractive prices.
Upper Pottinger Street is one of Hong Kong's traditional stepped 'ladder' streets which appear in old, sepia photographs of Central. Its tiny stalls specialise in haberdashery items of every description.
Walking further west along Queen's Road Central, beyond the rather smelly Central Market (selling fresh meat, live fish and poultry and vegetables), and on towards Queen's Road West, the visitor will encounter an area of small lanes to the left and right, where traditional Chinese life is in full swing, and a leisurely stroll in this area offers hours of intriguing exploration. Vendors selling the same goods cluster

Taste them if you dare ... an appetising display of 'hundred-year-old' eggs in Wing Sing Street

together—vegetable and fruit sellers, flower and plant stalls, rice stores, Chinese herbalists, feather merchants and ship's chandlers. At 109 Queen's Road Central stands one of Hong Kong's oldest traditional apothecaries, the **Eu Yan Sang Chinese Medicine Company**. Its walls are lined with medicine cabinets whose drawers and jars hold thousands of substances made from plants, minerals and animals. The dispensers deftly dispense prescriptions, weighing each ingredient, be it bear's gall, lizard powder, toad cake, ginseng or tiger's bone. China's rich medical tradition dates back several thousand years and is still very popular,

especially among the older generation. They feel that western medicine, though stronger, may have unknown side-effects, while the gentler Chinese concoctions are preventative in nature and accord with the natural body harmonies emphasised in Taoist thought. This store has a display of ingredients marked in English for anyone interested in the subject.

Wing On Street is known locally as 'Cloth Alley' for its fabrics and textiles galore. Each shop displays bolts of suiting, dress materials and furnishing fabrics—silk, velvet, cotton, rayon, wool and cashmere. Shop assistants speak English and will help you decide what lengths you should purchase for your blouse, skirt or jacket—and will bargain on the price.

The strong smell emanating from narrow little **Wing Sing Street** owes its origins to the tons of eggs which are sold here daily. Called colloquially 'Egg Street', its vendors deal in fresh hens' and ducks' eggs and 'hundred-year-old' preserved eggs. These are a Chinese delicacy always served with slices of pickled ginger. The ducks' eggs are buried in a mixture of lime, tea leaves and sawdust for several months, then coated with mud and rice-husks. This process turns the egg-white black, and eggs can be kept for up to six months.

The fresh eggs are counted and checked for freshness with amazing skill and swiftness. Some of the old vendors on the street can sometimes be heard singing an egg-counting ditty. Shops in the area of **Bonham Strand** and **Hillier Street** specialise in the health-restoring ginseng root, known as the 'king of medicinal herbs'. The most expensive ginseng is gathered wild in northeast China, and only a very small quantity is imported annually into Hong Kong as the cost runs into several hundred thousand Hong Kong dollars an ounce. It is believed to have the ability to prolong life and is administered to a dying person, thus gaining time for distant family members to gather at the bedside.

Tea merchants displaying beautiful painted caddies of Chinese tea and black cakes of popular *pu'er* tea, also sell little reddish-purple teapots made in Yixing, a town famous for its teaware in China's Jiangsu province.

Be careful not to open the wooden drawers in shops in this area for they may contain highly venomous live snakes. Snake shops import snakes from China and Thailand for medicinal purposes and for nourishing winter soups. The snake's gall-bladder is believed to be beneficial to rheumatism sufferers. The skilfully extracted raw gall-bladder is swallowed immediately and chastened with a cup of wine!

Upper Lascar Road, better known as Cat Street, is an antique flea market where anything you can think of, from wood carvings and jade jewellery to watches and electrical appliances, is laid out on the pavement for sale. Redevelopment of the area is, however, slowly encroaching upon Cat Street. This was a heavily populated Chinese neighbourhood in the latter part of the last century, and when bubonic plague swept through the colony for the first time in 1894, the population in this area suffered the worst effects. Seamen awaiting berths frequented the drinking and red-light establishments here, to the chagrin of missionaries, one of whom commented, in 1894, that 'they drink like fishes, ride round the town in rickshaws, making the night hideous with their shouts, eat over-ripe fruit from street stalls, are stricken with cholera and die in a few hours.'

On **Tai Ping Shan Street** are three little temples which date from the mid-19th century. The **Kuan-yin Temple** is frequented by women praying to the

Goddess of Mercy for the well-being of their children; at the Temple dedicated to the Pacifying General **Sui-tsing Paak** his healing forces are sought by worshippers. The **Paak Sing Temple** is dedicated to all ancestors, and means 'temple of a hundred surnames.' Over 3,000 commemorative soul tablets are kept here.

Hollywood Road is the centre of the antique trade and the shops display treasures and curios from all parts of southeast and northeast Asia. Artefacts include carved wooden furniture, golden gilded Buddhas, geometric neolithic pottery, sculpted stone

lions, antique paintings, *objets d'art* of jade and ivory, and fine blue and white Ming porcelain. Even if you have no intention of buying anything, browsing among these lovely antiques is a delight.

The large Taoist **Man Mo Temple** (126 Hollywood Road) dates from 1842 and, with its green tiled roof adorned with a frieze of porcelain figures, is a fine example of Chinese temple architecture. It is dedicated to the Civil God Man Cheong and the Military God Kwang Kung, whose statues stand side by side on the central altar. The air is pungent with the smoke and

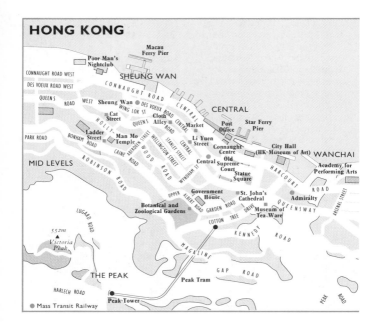

HONG KONG

fragrance of the huge, smouldering coils of incense which hang from the ceiling. There are always worshippers visiting the temple to pray, light candles and burn incense. The sounds of rustling bamboo fortune sticks and clacking wooden fortune blocks are an integral part of the mystical atmosphere which pervades this temple.

Lyndhurst Terrace also boasts antique shops, interspersed with picture framers and 'wedding shops'. The latter make the gorgeously elaborate traditional red Chinese wedding dresses, embroidered with sequins and beads, and golden jackets embossed with the queenly phoenix bird. They also make striking Chinese operatic costumes with accompanying high platformed boots and embroidered slippers. Towards the end of the last century, Lyndhurst Terrace became the address for a number of European brothels. Historical memoirs refer to the ostentatiously daring behaviour of one American 'lady of the night' who received payment in signed chits. She would attend church once a year and place her unpaid IOUs upon the collection plate.

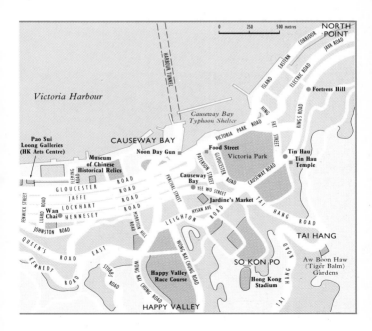

WHAT TO SEE

◆◆
BOTANICAL AND ZOOLOGICAL GARDENS
corner Upper Albert Road and Garden Road
The gardens were opened in 1871, and the zoo section built in 1975. The lush aviaries are home to hundreds of species of spectacular birds and the breeding programme here has been especially successful. A statue of Sir Arthur Kennedy, Governor of Hong Kong between 1872 and 1877, graces the gardens. This is a very popular spot for family weekend outings. The zoo and aviary sections are divided by Albany

The glass and steel headquarters of Hong Kong's largest bank – the Hong Kong & Shanghai Bank

Road, but are linked by an underground pass.

◆◆
CHATER GARDENS
Chater Road
These stand on the site of the old Hong Kong Cricket Club. The Club stood in the very heart of the business district until the 1960s, occupying possibly some of the most expensive real estate in the world! So seriously was the sport taken that young expatriate gentlemen were advised to bring their cricket shoes with them from England and from 1866 regular matches were played with members of the Shanghai Cricket Club. In 1892 the ship carrying the Shanghai team home floundered in the South China Sea and almost all the team drowned—a tragedy the Hong Kong Cricket Club

members took very much to heart.

Early each morning, office workers gather at Chater Gardens for traditional slow-movement *tai chi ch'uan* exercise classes.

♦♦♦
FLAGSTAFF HOUSE MUSEUM OF TEA WARE
Victoria Barracks (off Cotton Tree Drive)

Over 500 pieces of tea ware were presented by Dr K S Lo in the 1970s and this museum was created to house them in a delightful colonial style house, the oldest in Hong Kong.
Open: daily (except Wednesdays) 10.00–17.00.

♦♦
GOVERNMENT HOUSE
Upper Albert Road

The official residence and office of Hong Kong's Governor, the Queen's appointed representative. Government House was built in 1855–6 but the Japanese added the oriental tower, roof corners and the portico entrance during their occupation of Hong Kong between 1941 and 1945, considerably improving its appearance. During the 1967 riots and disturbances in Hong Kong—a political spill-over from the violence of the Cultural Revolution in China—pro-mainland demonstrators were a common sight parading round and round Government House waving Mao's 'little red book' of quotations. The gardens of Government House are thrown open to the public once a year, in spring, when the azaleas are in full bloom.

♦♦♦
HONG KONG MUSEUM OF ART
10th & 11th Floor, High Block, City Hall

The museum has an ever-growing collection of Chinese paintings, ceramics, bronzes, jade and embroideries which are augmented by private collections. Special exhibitions are held in the museum throughout the year.
Open: daily (except Thursdays) 10.00–18.00; Sundays and public holidays, 13.00–18.00.

♦♦♦
HONG KONG & SHANGHAI BANK
1 Queen's Road Central

The bank's 47-storey headquarters were designed by British architects, Foster Associates, and this is considered one of the most interesting ultra-modern glass and steel buildings in the world today. Requests to look round the building should be made to the bank.

The bank was founded by a group of China coast merchants in 1864 and has played a major role in Hong Kong's financial world ever since. It has occupied this site since the 1880s.

The three leading banks of the territory, the Chartered Bank, the Hong Kong & Shanghai Bank and the Bank of China, stood grandly side by side, since the 1930s, like imposing monoliths. Now only the old Bank of China, with its bronze Chinese guardian lions, remains for the present. Its new 70-storey home, designed by Chinese architect I M Pei, is being built near by.

OLD SUPREME COURT
Statue Square
Constructed in the first decade of the century, this building housed the Supreme Court until 1985, when it became the territory's Legislative Council Chambers. Built in granite with tall Ionic pillars and a pinnacled dome, it typifies the English School of architecture and was designed by a leading British architect of the period, Aston Webb. It remains one of the few western-style old buildings to be preserved.

ST JOHN'S CATHEDRAL
Garden Road
The Victorian Gothic-style cathedral dates from 1849, when its Anglican diocese included Hong Kong, China, Japan and Korea. During World War II, the Japanese used the cathedral as an officers' club. The damage was extensive; all the early stained glass windows were lost, as were many of the memorial tablets. Money for the restoration of the cathedral after the war was raised by private and company contributions. It is a peaceful haven in the midst of high-rise Hong Kong. Lunchtime concerts are held in the cathedral once a week.
The nearby red brick building at the top of Battery Path has had a very strange history. Built in the 1880s it first served as a junior mess for young bankers and traders, then as the Russian Consulate, before housing the **French Mission**, which was active in missionary work throughout Asia. Later the

Education Department occupied it, and then the Victoria District Court. It is now designated to be the headquarters of the Joint Liaison Group, which is concerned with the 1997 return of Hong Kong to China.

STATUE SQUARE
between Des Voeux Road and Chater Road
A small haven of green in downtown Central District, in which stands a statue of the Chief Manager of the Hong Kong & Shanghai Bank from 1876 to 1902. This area is the favourite haunt on weekends for thousands of Filipino maids who enjoy their day off work chatting and meeting with their colleagues. Near by is the **War Memorial Cenotaph** and beside it the premises of the **Hong Kong Club**—'once the paradise of the select, and temple of colonial gentility'. Today's modern structure replaced an elegant rococo façaded building built in 1898. Its demolition in the late 1970s was a source of much distress to those who fight the battle to preserve Hong Kong's architectural heritage.

VICTORIA PEAK
A trip to 'The Peak' on the Peak Tram is an essential part of any visitor's stay, for the ride itself is an experience (seats on the right hand side of the tram offer the best views) as the tram rises steeply up the mountain side, making the high-rise apartment blocks appear to be built on an angle. From the top the views are superb day or night. The circular restaurant on top of the

A view of Hong Kong from the top of exclusive Victoria Peak

tram terminus has a panoramic view and serves a good buffet each lunchtime.

In the mid 19th century Europeans took to building summer houses on Victoria Peak, 1,806ft (554m) high, and it became a place where 'one can spend a summer in Hong Kong with a reasonable probability of being alive at the end of it'. Elegant colonial houses sprang up along the ridges of Victoria Peak, Mount Gough and Mount Kellett, and in the 1870s the Governor, too, had a summer residence built here. Chinese were not permitted to build on the Peak until the turn of the century.

Access to the Peak, until the Peak Tram's construction in 1888, was by sedan chair, carried by relays of coolies. One eccentric resident of the Peak rode a camel! The Peak Road was completed only in 1924. Today an address on the Peak still has an élitist cachet, even though for some months of the year residents are shrouded in gloomy mist and cloud. Rents on the Peak can run to HK$80,000 a month.

A number of long scenic walks begin here but more leisurely and spectacular is the walk around Victoria Peak, along Lugard and Harlech Roads. It takes only 45 minutes and is quite flat. From this circular walk, among delightful semi-tropical vegetation, wide views of the eastern and western approaches to Victoria Harbour and across to the Kowloon peninsula are enjoyed, while Aberdeen and the islands of Lamma and Cheung Chau on the southern side of the island also come into view.

WESTERN DISTRICT

To the west of Central District, dried fish wholesalers dominate **Des Voeux Road West** in **Sai Ying Pun**, and the visitor's senses are assailed by the sights and smells of the merchandise— squid, fish, sea cucumbers, oysters, shrimp, jelly fish and abalone. Other delicacies, such as dried chrysanthemum flowers, red dates, dried mushrooms, lotus seeds and pickles are also sold. In the streets behind, wholesalers deal in sharks' fins and birds' nests— luxury items even for the rich Chinese. On **Queen's Road West** it is still possible to find professional roadside letter-writers. There are said to be about 70 licensed letter-writers in Hong Kong. They are usually men, and their customers are normally elderly women with

Calligraphy, developed in 200BC when the writing brush was invented, is one of the greatest of Chinese arts

families abroad or on the mainland, with whom they wish to communicate. These calligraphers are in high demand at Chinese New Year to write red-paper auspicious couplets, which are pasted on the doorway of each Chinese home.

WHAT TO SEE

◆◆
HONG KONG UNIVERSITY
Bonham Road
Established in 1912, the University now has over 8,000 students studying arts, architecture, dentistry, education, engineering, law, medicine, science and social sciences. Competition for places in this English language University is fierce. One of its most famous students was the Chinese revolutionary Dr Sun Yat-sen (1866–1925), father of modern China, who received his degree in 1892 from the College of Medicine which formed the core of the University. The original building, Loke Yew Hall, is built in Renaissance style around a quiet garden courtyard, and surmounted by a clock-tower and turrets. The **Fung Ping Shan Museum** building, built in 1932, first served as the University's library before housing the Fung family art collection. The collection now consists mainly of early Shang, Chou and Han bronzes, neolithic pottery, glazed tomb figures and porcelains from China's famous kilns. The museum has the world's largest collection of Yuan dynasty Nestorian crosses (open Monday to Saturday 09.30–18.00).

One of the fascinations of Hong Kong is the food – to eat or just to look at. This Western District stall specialises in dried food

◆
KENNEDY TOWN
Reached by tram, Kennedy Town offers a glimpse of the busy waterfront where junks and lighters load and unload cargoes from China. It is named after Governor Sir Arthur Kennedy (1872–7) during whose tenure wharves were built along the waterfront and middle-class Chinese merchants and craftsmen resided in the area. Take the tram all the way to Western and walk around Kennedy Town's market streets.

EASTERN DISTRICT

The territory to the east of
Central District takes in the
areas of Wanchai, Happy Valley,
Causeway Bay, North Point and
Shau Kei Wan.

WHAT TO SEE

◆◆◆
CAUSEWAY BAY

Prices in this busy shopping area
are lower than in Central
District. Big Japanese
department stores and a branch
of China Products are to be
found here. A popular local
market in the area is **Jardine's
Bazaar**. One end overflows with
cheap clothing stalls—blouses,
jeans, underwear—and the
other with fresh meat,
vegetables, fruits and flowers.
On the waterfront, opposite the
Excelsior Hotel, stands Hong
Kong's **Noonday Gun** which
Noël Coward made famous in his
song *Mad Dogs and Englishmen*:
'In Hong Kong they strike a gong
and fire off the noonday gun'.
The custom had grown of giving
the *taipan* (a name by which the
heads of the major China coast
trading companies are known) of
Jardine, Matheson & Co an
official send-off with a 21-gun
salute. Annoyed by this
arrogance, the Navy directed
the company, as a punishment, to
fire the gun at noon each day
until further notice. The custom
continued until World War II
when the cannon was rendered
useless. After the war the Royal
Navy provided another cannon,
which, in accordance with this
odd little tradition, is fired at
noon each day and on midnight
of New Year's Eve.

*The gardens that Aw Boon Haw built
are full of statues and grottos*

The **typhoon shelter** is the
permanent home of a number of
boat dwellers as well as a haven
for small boats when typhoons
threaten. During the summer
months sampans can be hired in
the evening but they are
unlicensed and unhygienic. Fresh
seafood and noodles can be
ordered from 'kitchen boats'. Music
boats will entertain you while
you eat, once the price is agreed.
This can be an expensive
evening. To reach the typhoon

shelter, walk over the overpass near Victoria Park.

Causeway Bay abounds in eating establishments. **Food Street** is a special attraction where restaurants serve Japanese, Chinese, Vietnamese, Korean and western food and the fountained arcade makes a pleasant atmosphere in which to make a decision on where to eat.

Victoria Park is one of the few open spaces in this built-up area and bird-lovers like to hang their elegantly caged songsters on the branches of the park's trees. There are a number of sports

facilities in the park, and on Sundays it often becomes a forum for public meetings where local issues are voiced. People like to practise the martial art of *kung fu* or the sedate *tai chi ch'uan* movements here in the early mornings. A Flower Fair is held annually in the park at Chinese New Year. The statue of Queen Victoria which graces the park was created in 1895.

The 'Tiger Balm' cure-all ointment millionaire, Aw Boon Haw, built the **Aw Boon Haw Gardens** in 1935 on Tai Hang Road. He filled the steep eight-acre hillside above Causeway Bay with plaster statues which depict the whole range of Buddhist and Chinese mythology, much of it quite gruesome, especially the depiction of the tortures carried out in the afterworld's Ten Courts of Hell. The six-storey Tiger Pagoda is a distinctive landmark. The Aw family has a remarkable collection of jade, which may also be viewed.

Open: 10.00 to 16.00, admission free.

MTR Subway: Causeway Bay Station.

HAPPY VALLEY

Horse racing has been part of Hong Kong's sporting life—more as a passion than a sport—almost since the acquisition of the island by the British. The Happy Valley Race Course was created in 1845 when horses were imported from Shanghai and northern China. One of Hong Kong's Governors, Sir Henry May (1912–1919), was both an

Racing fans flock to the Happy Valley Race Course, which is less than a mile (1.6km) long

owner and a jockey! During a race meeting in 1918 the race stand caught fire and in the ensuing disaster 600 people perished.

Early attempts at settlement of Happy Valley were equally disastrous. In the early 1840s soldiers quartered here fell prey to malaria and the area soon became known as the 'White Man's Grave'. Even after extensive draining was carried out, epidemics continued to decimate the European population. Little wonder that the **Colonial Cemetery** was established here in 1845. The gravestones in this gently tended garden bear the names of many who were prominent in Hong Kong's early history and are a witness to the precariousness of life in the east—some died in typhoons, some at the hands of pirates and many of fever and plagues. John Le Carré recreates the cemetery in scenes from his book *The Honourable Schoolboy*.

◆◆
NORTH POINT TO SHAU KEI WAN

Three districts lie east of Causeway Bay: North Point, Quarry Bay and Shau Kei Wan. In *The Hong Kong Guide*, published in 1893, the disenchanted writer makes the comment: 'The road to Shau-ki Wan was the Rotten Row of the Colony in those stupid days when everyone thought himself bound to keep a carriage, whether he could afford it or not, and the sole amusement was solemnly driving along this

weary road every afternoon!' Today these districts are principally high density residential areas comprised of both government and private low-cost housing estates. The Shanghainese clannishly settled in **North Point** and it is therefore also called Little Shanghai. Not surprisingly most of the restaurants here serve Shanghainese food.

Quarry Bay continues its industrial tradition. Dockyards were founded here in 1863 and later Butterfield & Swire, one of the leading Far Eastern trading companies which ran ships up and down the China coast and along the lower Yangtse River, built their Taikoo Dockyard in 1908. The Taikoo Sugar Refinery, also a part of the B & S empire, had already been constructed in Quarry Bay in 1882. The huge Taikoo Shing housing estate now stands on this redeveloped site, and the dockyards occupy a much smaller area.

Shau Kei Wan, at the eastern end of the island, in 1841 only a fishing village with a population of 1,200, still keeps its seagoing tradition. It is the homebase for a large fishing fleet, second only in importance to Aberdeen. Perhaps because of the poverty of its early villagers, or because it was prey to piratical attacks, the area was known as 'the Bay of Hungry Men'.

There are two temples of interest: the **Tin Hau Temple** on Main Street, dedicated to the Goddess of the Sea and built around 1874; and the **Tam Kung Temple** at the end of Main Street on the waterfront. On the eighth day of the fourth moon (May) the fishing community holds boisterous birthday celebrations for Tam Kung, a deity who is believed to control the elements, especially typhoons. A beautiful 150-ft (45m) silk dragon dances down Main Street, paying its respects to all the business premises. Lively lion dances go on outside the temple throughout the day. It is a festival well worth attending. Dragon boat races are also held at Shau Kei Wan during the Dragon Boat Festival (see **Special Events**, page 106). Take the tram from Central to Shau Kei Wan and catch the MTR subway back.

WANCHAI

Wanchai is famous for its nightlife and 'girlie' bars, and never more so than during the Vietnam War when American servicemen came to Hong Kong for rest and recreation. Mention of Wanchai immediately brings to mind the film *The World of Suzie Wong*, a poignant love story of one such bar girl. During the Japanese occupation (1941–45), Wanchai was designated a red-light district, and many of the bar girls were Japanese. The bright lights, night clubs and topless bars always attract a clientele, either regular or curious.

But Wanchai is also a respectable residential area, one of the oldest in fact, designated for Chinese occupation in the 1840s. Refugees from the bloody Tai Ping Rebellion on the mainland flooded into the area during the 1850s and large squatter areas resulted. British military barracks were established in Wanchai, just east of Central, and it wasn't long before brothels followed suit. A number of early missionary societies and church institutions built hospitals, mission houses and orphanages. Wanchai still has the flavour of pre-war Hong Kong, with typical old four-storey tenements, sometimes with wrought-iron balconies and bamboo washing poles in evidence. But these too are slowly falling under the developers' hammers. As in Central, Queen's Road formed the waterfront in Wanchai too, but reclamation during the 1930s extended the area to Gloucester Road. More recent reclamation has created valuable waterfront land for office accommodation, hotels, exhibition and arts centres, sports grounds and lighter cargo handling facilities. Walking the small streets between Queen's Road East and Johnston Road the visitor will find street markets stocked with fresh vegetables and fruit, bird shops, clothing vendors, and pavement restaurants. You may also find people fortune telling, an occupation often practised by the blind.

On Queen's Road East the small **Hung Shing Temple**, with its carved granite balustrade, dates from the 1860s, while its Shek Wan pottery roof decorations are turn of the century. The big stone, around which the temple is built, is believed to have been a shrine even prior to the arrival of the British. Hung Shing is one of the patron saints of the seafarers. Near by, still on Queen's Road East, is the quaint little **Wanchai Post Office**, built in 1915—the

Despite its changing face, the Wanchai red-light district is still famed for its nightlife

oldest one still surviving. Close by is the 66-storey high **Hopewell Centre**, one of the landmarks of Wanchai; at the top is a revolving restaurant. There are several other temples in the vicinity, including the **Sui Tsing Pak** on Tik Lung Lane, which houses some interesting antiques, and the **Pak Tai Temple** off Stone Nullah Lane, dedicated to the God of the North and built in the 1860s. *MTR subway*: Wanchai Station. **The Museum of Chinese Historical Relics**, on the first floor of the Causeway Centre, exhibits cultural treasures from China which include paintings and handicrafts; occasional exhibitions only (open daily 10.00–18.00). And in the Hong Kong Arts Centre, Harbour Road, the **Pao Sui Loong Galleries** hold regular exhibitions with particular emphasis on modern art (open daily 10.00–20.00).

SOUTHERN DISTRICT

A trip along the southern coast of Hong Kong Island is well worthwhile. Several popular venues lie along this coast, as well as a number of beaches.

WHAT TO SEE

◆◆◆
ABERDEEN

Aberdeen's image has changed vastly in recent years—from a small fishing harbour to a modern urban centre.
Fishing is still a major industry and the harbour is busy with deep-sea fishing boats. Many Tanka boat people still live aboard junks, and sampan ladies importune tourists with offers of half-hour boat rides (pay around HK$50) to see this astonishing floating world. The junks are quite spacious and there is room for family pets, chicken coops, drying fish and the essential TV set. Sampans selling groceries, vegetables and fruit supply the floating housewife with her daily needs. The larger boats are fitted with radar and make fishing expeditions into the South China Sea for several weeks at a time. At Chinese New Year and the Dragon Boat Festival the harbour is packed with boats bedecked with multi-coloured flags and streaming banners. Sampan rides around the harbour are fun, and offer a staggering glimpse of the contrasts of Hong Kong's society. Your boat skims round and about the floating homes and then out to the vast floating restaurants, for which Aberdeen is so famous. These are moored beside the opulent Aberdeen

Once a typhoon shelter and harbour, Aberdeen is now a floating tourist attraction

Marina where the rich have their pleasure boats.
Aberdeen's **Tin Hau Temple** is dedicated to the Queen of Heaven, protectress of fisherfolk, and was built in 1851 on what was then the water's edge. The frieze of pottery figures on the roof is charming. There are two

large cast-metal bells on either side of the entrance, one dated 1726 and said to have been found in the sea, and the other dated 1851. The Goddess takes centre stage on the altar, flanked by two life-size military generals, one who can hear clearly and one who can see clearly for one thousand *li*—about 300 miles (480km). But perhaps the most popular shrine in Aberdeen, frequented daily by fishing women burning incense and little paper boats, lies a little to the east of the bus terminal on the waterfront. It comprises several small smoke-blackened shrines at the base of an old tree. Chinese herbalists do well in Aberdeen among the more traditional and conservative fishing community and apart from the array of pharmacopoeia in the shops there are many individual street herbalists, some of them practising moxibustion (a form of heat cupping). The sale of fishing tackle is also an important retail business in this area.

On the island of **Ap Lei Chau**, on the other side of Aberdeen harbour, traditional boat building techniques are still used in the dockyards. Ap Lei Chau can be reached by a linking bridge, built in 1979, or by shuttle ferry. Aberdeen is world famous for its gigantic floating restaurants. Shuttle services to the three restaurants—Jumbo, Sea Palace and Tai Pak—operate from Aberdeen Main Pier or from Shum Wan Ferry Pier

(bus no 90 or 97 from the Central Bus Terminal).

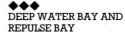

DEEP WATER BAY AND REPULSE BAY

The scenery on the southern side of the island is quietly spectacular and the beaches of Deep Water Bay and Repulse Bay are crowded during the summer bathing season with swimmers and barbecue parties. Repulse Bay is called in Chinese 'Shallow Water Bay', which is a

Repulse Bay Temple is a colourful feature in an area where the beach is the main crowd-puller during the summer

true geographical description of this pretty bay, named after HMS *Repulse*, which pursued local pirates. The colonial-style Repulse Bay Hotel once overlooked the bay, but this was unfortunately pulled down in the redevelopment frenzy. So popular was its elegant veranda restaurant that a replica has been constructed. It is a delightful place to take afternoon tea. British troops occupied the hotel in the face of the Japanese advance around the island and engaged them in battle within the walls of the old hotel—one of the classic incidents in the fall of the island in 1941. The British commander later recalled of the event: 'We rolled . . . grenades along the beautifully carpeted corridor for all the world as if we'd been in a bowling alley.'

◆◆◆
OCEAN PARK

Ocean Park covers 170 hillside acres with gardens, aviaries, oceanarium, atoll reef aquaria, and penguin and sea lion wave pool. Seals, sea lions, dolphins and killer whales perform daily at the ocean theatre, which accommodates 3,500 people. A scenic cable car services the upper headland in a breathtaking 8–10-minute ride. Opened in 1977, it has proved a great success both for locals and tourists.

Open: weekdays from 10.00 to 18.00, and Sundays and holidays from 09.00 to 18.00. Admission is half-price for children.

Water World, next door to Ocean Park, has exciting, stomach-heaving water games and swimming facilities.

STANLEY

Stanley lies on the south side of the island, about 10 minutes by road beyond Repulse Bay. It is one of the island's oldest settlements; when the British came in 1841 the population was around 2,000, and it was one of the first British military bases to be established on Hong Kong Island. At the fall of Hong Kong the men of the Middlesex and Royal Rifles Regiments made a heroic stand against the Japanese, side by side with Volunteer gunners, at horrible cost. A brutal civilian internment camp was established at the Stanley Prison by the Japanese and the small military cemetery, which dates from the 1840s, is a grim reminder of that suffering. The British Military continues to occupy part of the Stanley peninsula but this is a restricted area.

Most visitors come here to bargain hunt for designer sportswear, jeans, silk garments and knick-knacks in the shops and stalls of **Stanley Market**. A lot of delving and rummaging is necessary, and the fitting rooms are minute, but it can be a fun shopping experience. Just walk down Stanley Market Street from the bus stop and you can't miss it. There are also two good swimming beaches: **Stanley Main Beach** and **St Stephen's Beach**.

At the end of Stanley Main Street stands the 18th-century **Tin Hau Temple**, the oldest temple on Hong Kong Island. Inside the temple, dedicated to the Queen of Heaven, stands a bell and drum which belonged to the

Old village houses can still be seen among Stanley's high-rise blocks

pirate Chang Po Chai, who signalled his ships with them. A rather tatty tiger's skin hangs on one of the walls, shot near the temple by a Japanese soldier during the occupation. A forbidding array of black and gold temple gods stands on a stone ledge which runs around three sides of the temple. This is an unusual feature. Tin Hau herself is richly arrayed and the altar reverently curtained. Beyond the Tin Hau temple, situated along the water's edge, is a squatter area soon to be cleared (bus no 6 and 260 from Exchange Square Bus Terminal go to Repulse Bay and Stanley: a journey of about 45 minutes). The beaches at **Shek O** and **Big Wave Bay** around the eastern side of Hong Kong Island are also popular during the weekends.

KOWLOON

In 1860 the tip of Kowloon peninsula, 4 square miles (12 sq km), was ceded to Britain in a very unorthodox fashion. The British negotiators gave a handful of earth wrapped in paper to the Chinese mandarin officials. They in turn handed it back, signifying cession. The area then comprised 10 villages with a population of about 5,000. In 1898 a lease of 99 years on 380 extra square miles (981 sq km) was agreed upon, which included the New Territories. The name Kowloon means Nine Dragons, after the nine peaks which range behind it. In the 13th century the last of the southern Sung dynasty emperors, a boy-emperor, found a happy refuge here briefly before being drowned off the coast of Lantau Island shortly after. It is said that the young emperor was only able to count eight Dragon peaks and a courtier retorted that the boy himself, a descendant of the Dragon throne, was the ninth. Most of the hills have now disappeared and those that are left, especially those glimpsed to the east of Kai Tak Airport, are starkly denuded; this deforestation was carried out during the Japanese occupation. The possession of Kowloon peninsula was strategically important, as it secured the Victoria Harbour anchorage from attack by Imperial Chinese batteries. The British built a number of barracks and moved their soldiers from earlier military settlements on Hong Kong Island.

At first the expatriates built holiday homes in Kowloon and it was not until the turn of the century that development took a serious turn. One of the first communities to establish residence here was that of the Portuguese, who built their own Catholic Rosary Church on Chatham Road in 1905. Later they moved to the suburb of Kowloon Tong which even today is the only truly 'suburban' district in Hong Kong where residents actually live in houses with gardens.

The districts of San Po Kong, Kwun Tong and Kowloon Bay are principally industrial. On multi-storeyed factory premises, silk garments, electronic components, cotton cloth, toys, electrical appliances, watches, etc, are manufactured for export markets.

WHAT TO SEE

LAI CHI KOK DISTRICT
The Sung Dynasty Village on Lai King Hill Road is a charming representation of life in China during one of its richest periods (960–1279). Skilled wood-carvers were brought from China to re-create the architecture while traditionally costumed 'villagers' add to the atmosphere. Visitors to the 60,000 square foot (5,600 sq m) village are shown a traditional wedding ceremony, acrobatics, and martial arts demonstrations. Calligraphers wield their hair brushes and skilled craftsmen show how to roll incense sticks, make rice paper, and flour noodles. A restaurant serves meals or snacks as musicians

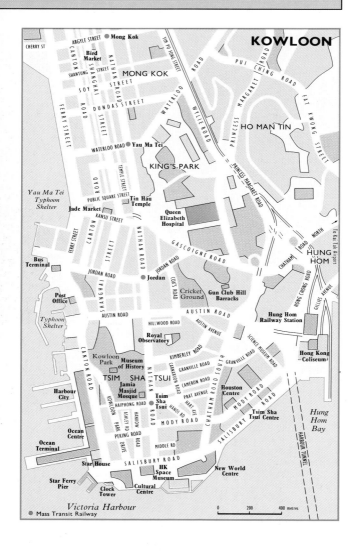

KOWLOON

CHERRY ST

ARGYLE STREET ● Mong Kok

Bird Market

MONG KOK

CANTON ROAD

SHANGHAI STREET

NATHAN ROAD

SHANTUNG STREET

SOY STREET

DUNDAS STREET

FERRY STREET

TIN PO YONG STREET

WATERLOO ROAD

WYLIE ROAD

PUI CHING ROAD

FAT KWONG STREET

PRINCESS MARGARET ROAD

HO MAN TIN

PRINCESS MARGARET ROAD

WATERLOO ROAD ● Yau Ma Tei

KING'S PARK

TEMPLE STREET

PUBLIC SQUARE STREET

Yau Ma Tei Typhoon Shelter

Jade Market

Tin Hau Temple

KANSU STREET

CANTON ROAD

SHANGHAI STREET

NATHAN ROAD

Queen Elizabeth Hospital

GASCOIGNE ROAD

CHATHAM ROAD NORTH

To Kai Tak Airport

HUNG HOM

Bus Terminal

FERRY STREET

JORDAN ROAD

● Jordan

JORDAN ROAD

COX'S ROAD

Cricket Ground

Gun Club Hill Barracks

HONG CHONG ROAD

GILLIES AVENUE

Post Office

Typhoon Shelter

AUSTIN ROAD

AUSTIN ROAD

HILLWOOD ROAD

AUSTIN AVENUE

Hung Hom Railway Station

Royal Observatory

KIMBERLEY ROAD

SCIENCE MUSEUM ROAD

Hong Kong Coliseum

CANTON ROAD

Kowloon Park

Museum of History

NATHAN ROAD

CARNARVON ROAD

GRANVILLE ROAD

GRANVILLE ROAD

TSIM SHA TSUI

Jamia Masjid Mosque

KOWLOON PARK

HAIPHONG ROAD

Tsim Sha Tsui ●

CAMERON ROAD

PRAT AVENUE

HART AVE.

Houston Centre

MODY ROAD

CHATHAM ROAD SOUTH

Tsim Sha Tsui Centre

Harbour City

ASHLEY RD

HANKOW ROAD

HANOI RD

MODY ROAD

Hung Hom Bay

Ocean Centre

PEKING ROAD

DRIVE

MIDDLE RD

SALISBURY ROAD

HARBOUR TUNNEL

Ocean Terminal

Star House

SALISBURY ROAD

HK Space Museum

New World Centre

Star Ferry Pier

Clock Tower

Cultural Centre

Victoria Harbour

● Mass Transit Railway

0   200   400 metres

Kowloon, or 'Nine Dragons', was named in the 13th century; Sung Dynasty Village recreates that period

play Chinese folk songs. Coupons are available to buy small delicacies. The Sung Village is organised around daily group tours but it is open to individuals between 12.30 and 17.00 (bus no 6A from Kowloon Star Ferry to the last bus stop). **Lai Chi Kok Amusement Park**, Lai King Hill Road, though a typical fun-fair park, is an excellent place to watch Chinese Opera, for there are evening performances between 19.00 and 20.00.

Another site in the area is the **Lei Cheung Uk Tomb and Museum**, 41 Tonkin Street, Sham Shui Po. The Han Dynasty burial vault (AD22–220) was discovered in 1955 during site work for a government housing estate. The tomb itself (four brick chambers in the form of a cross) and tomb objects are on display (open daily, except Thursdays, 10.00– 13.00 and 14.00–18.00; Sundays and public holidays 13.00–18.00).

◆◆
TSIM SHA TSUI DISTRICT

Tsim Sha Tsui, meaning Sharp, Sandy Point, is the heart of Kowloon's commercial and tourist district. Its shopping centres, hotels and restaurants are a visitors' mecca. The main tree-lined thoroughfare is **Nathan Road**, running for 3 miles (5km) in a north-south axis. When constructed at the turn of the century it was called

Nathan's Folly, after Governor Sir Matthew Nathan (1904–1907), whose pet project it was. It was seen as both unnecessary and an extravagance. Now the Tsim Sha Tsui section is known more affectionately as 'the Golden Mile'. Off Nathan Road runs a web of streets, ablaze with shop signs in Chinese and English, which offer just about everything a person could wish for. Major shopping complexes include the Ocean Terminal, on the waterfront beside the Star Ferry. This converges with Ocean Centre to create a huge shopping and hotel area along Canton Road which is always busy with shoppers, and never more so than on Sundays, when Hong Kong people do their browsing and purchasing. The New World Centre on Salisbury Road is another striking example of an up-market shopping paradise.

Shop signs vie for attention in the tourist area of Tsim Sha Tsui

The **Hong Kong Museum of History** on Haiphong Road concentrates on local history, with changing exhibitions on subjects such as traditional village life, fishing craft, marriage customs and archaeology (open daily, except Fridays, 10.00–18.00; Sundays and public holidays 13.00–18.00). At 10 Salisbury Road the **Space Museum** offers a Space Theatre, with lecture halls and dazzling special effects (closed Tuesdays).

The newest tourist area is **East Tsim Sha Tsui** where many new hotels—Shangri-la, Regal Meridien, Royal Garden and Holiday Inn Harbour View—are situated and supported by restaurants and shopping malls. The area was developed on the site of the old marshalling yards of the Kowloon–Canton Railway. Like Hong Kong, the best way to see the area is on foot.

By the Star Ferry stands a **Clock Tower** which has been preserved as a monument to the old Kowloon–Canton Railway station built in 1916. The old station stood on this site until 1978 and travellers could board a train here and journey all the way to Europe, through China, Mongolia and Russia. Close to completion on the vacated site is a new cultural complex, whose design has been much criticised, for it stands on one of the prime sites in all of Hong Kong and does not have a single window! A walk along the **Tsim Sha Tsui Promenade**, between the Space Museum and East Tsim Sha Tsui, presents a grand vista of Victoria Harbour with its ferries, yachts, tugs, junks, pleasure launches,

lighters, liners, hydrofoils and visiting warships. At night the scene is equally breathtaking against the backdrop of Hong Kong's neon-lit outline.

Another landmark is the élitist **Peninsula Hotel** on Salisbury Road, opposite the Space Museum. Built in 1925 in grand colonial style to cater for international travellers, it found its spacious rooms occupied by troops after the government requisitioned the hotel during the crisis year of 1925, when Hong Kong had a general strike and boycott of British goods. Hong Kong's Chinese workers supported their compatriots in the foreign concessions of Shanghai and Canton where labour demonstrations had taken an anti-foreign turn and ended in machine-gun massacres. Officially opened in 1928, the hotel went into business only to be requisitioned by Japanese officers during the occupation. The Governor, Sir Mark Young, conceded the surrender of Hong Kong in front of the hotel in 1941. Afternoon tea or cocktails in the ornate gold and white foyer of the Peninsula Hotel is a must if you like to sit back and people-watch.

The distinctive Islamic architecture of **Jamia Masjid Mosque**—on the corner of Nathan and Haiphong Road—may seem oddly incongruous in Hong Kong, but there are over 50,000 Muslims in the territory, most of them Chinese. Islam was introduced to China around the 7th century by Arab traders. A mosque has occupied this site since 1896. To visit the mosque, first telephone 7240095.

TSUEN WAN

The **Sam Tung Uk** (walled village) museum is a mid-18th century Hakka village which belonged to the Chan clan. It has survived the growth of the industrial satellite town of Tsuen Wan and has been landscaped, restored and converted to a delightful folk museum, with permanent exhibitions of farming implements and furniture (open daily 09.00–16.00; closed Tuesdays).
MTR subway: Tsuen Wan Station.

◆◆
WONG TAI SIN DISTRICT

The large modern **Wong Tai Sin Temple** stands in a high-rise government housing estate on Lung Cheung Road and was built in the early 1970s. Wong Tai Sin is said to have been a young shepherd when he was taken by an immortal and taught how to make an elixir of immortality. Today his followers believe him to be able to cure illness as well as bestowing luck at the races. Beside the temple are fortune tellers' stalls displaying their physiognomy and palmistry charts as enticements. The physiognomists work from classical reference books which were first written in the Sung (960–1126) and Ch'ing (1644–1908) dynasties, although the art is mentioned in histories of the 2nd century BC.
MTR Subway: Wong Tai Sin Station.

◆◆◆
YAU MA TEI & MONG KOK DISTRICTS

One of the many curious sights in

Wong Tai Sin Temple is dedicated to a god only introduced to Hong Kong as recently as 1915

Hong Kong is the **Bird Market** on Hong Lok Street (Mong Kok MTR station). Chinese greatly prize singing birds, and pay high prices for a good songster. Finely crafted bird cages and delicate little porcelain feeding bowls can also demand high

items on sale in their shops: sequined Chinese wedding dresses, bamboo steamers, gold ornaments, mahjong sets, snakes, fragrant incense and temple ware.

Jade Market is found under the Gascoigne Road flyover on Kansu Street, Yau Ma Tei (take MTR to Jordan Road station). The dealers display trays of carved jade pendants, rings, bracelets and ornaments. But unless you know something about jade, just buy for pleasure and enjoy bargaining. Serious Chinese buyers can be seen negotiating secret deals using sign language. A translucent green jade bracelet is traditionally bought by Chinese women to celebrate the birth of a son. Chinese hold jade in the highest esteem and Confucius wrote: 'It is soft, smooth and shining like kindness; it is hard, fine and strong, like intelligence; its edges seem sharp, but do not cut, like justice; it hangs down to the ground like humility; when struck, it gives a clear, ringing sound, like music; the stains in it which are not hidden and add to its beauty are like truthfulness; its brightness is like heaven, while its firm substance, born of mountains and the water, is like the earth.'

The market is open from 10.00 to 15.30 daily.

Temple Street Market, Temple Street, Yau Ma Tei, springs to life each night between 20.00 and 23.00. This colourful and lively market sells cheap clothing, with the emphasis on men's wear. Its food stalls, story tellers and fortune tellers reading palms and faces, make this an

prices. There are hundreds of imported birds on sale each day. On the corner of Shanghai and Soy Streets is the **Wan Loy Teahouse**, where each morning at 06.30 bird lovers sip tea and appreciate their songbirds, hanging the cages from bamboo poles.

Canton Road and **Shanghai Street**, west of Jordan Road, both present an absorbing array of

interesting night excursion.
Tin Hau Temple near Public Square Street (close to the Jade Market) in Yau Ma Tei, although dedicated to the Queen of Heaven, has a number of other deities under the same roof. In its four halls are statues of the City God, God of Earth, the Goddess of Mercy and the God of Justice. Worshippers at the temple, built about 120 years ago, are mostly boat people from the nearby typhoon shelter. Red-robed Taoist monks officiate at special services and the temple is always busy with devout believers. The wall of one of the halls is lined with 60 gods, wrapped in red paper—one for each year of the Chinese 60-year cycle.

A fine way to see the sights

Yau Ma Tei Typhoon Shelter on Ferry Street (Yau Ma Tei MTR station) is home to many Hoklo and Tanka boat people whose traditional fishing grounds are the south China coast. They speak different dialects and practise their own customs. Many of the long term residents in the typhoon shelter work ashore and anxiously await government housing; but it is still a self-contained community with a clinic, school and sampan merchants. Along the waterfront a procession of lighters and junks load and unload their cargoes.

In the streets behind Ferry Street, lying south of Waterloo Road, there are wood-carvers' shops making decorated Chinese deities, as well as mahjong houses.

NEW TERRITORIES

Until some 20 years ago the New Territories, leased to Britain in 1898 for 99 years, were still mainly agricultural, the villagers leading a traditional rural lifestyle growing crops of vegetables and rice. Very few pockets of this old society exist today, and less rice is grown. The paddy fields lie fallow and overgrown, simply awaiting an offer from a suitable real estate developer. Many of the older villagers live on remittances from relatives living and working overseas, and spend their time in tea houses gossiping and playing mahjong.

The rapid development of vast high rise towns has completely changed the nature of the area, and vast roadworks are underway to deal with the ever-growing cross-border traffic with China. The electrification of the Kowloon–Canton Railway has put the New Territories into the commuter belt. By 1990 one-third of Hong Kong's population will have been rehoused here. The land was settled by five main Chinese clans, who are Cantonese speaking and known as Punti or 'locals'. Their clan connections lay in nearby Guangdong province, and they began arriving between the 12th and 14th centuries, settling first in the rich flats in the northwest of the New Territories around Tuen Mun, Yuen Long, San Tin and Sheung Shui. The Hakka (which means 'guest' or 'tenant') came to the area only in the 17th century, settling in the eastern part of the New Territories and speaking their own dialect. The Hakka women wear distinctive round straw hats hung with a black frill and are frequently seen working on construction sites.

During the mid 17th century the south China coast was infested with pirates who terrorised the inhabitants. Emperor Kang Hsi ordered a coastal evacuation of all villages in 1661, so as to deny supplies and information to the pirates. The clans suffered enormously as a result and when they were eventually allowed back to their lands a decade later, they were much depleted in numbers. They took on the Hakkas as tenant farmers.

When the British leased the New Territories there were about 700 extant villages. A village was sited according to the geomantic principles of *feng shui* (wind and rain), which usually meant building houses close together at the foot of a hill and just above the paddy fields, cramming them into parallel terraces with narrow access lanes. Trees were planted to deflect negative *feng shui* influences and protect the village. Even with such enormous consideration given to the siting of a village there could be problems. At Sun Uk Village, for instance, the first position was found to be very propitious for accumulating wealth but not for the birth of male children. The demand for male progeny outweighed all other needs, and the clan moved to another site. Boundaries of villages were also often set according to *feng shui* needs and this caused inter-village strife.

Clans built ancestral halls in their villages in accordance with the

Confucian ethics of filial piety and ancestral worship, and these are still used at special clan celebrations. The tablets of the ancestors are kept here (immediate ancestors are also worshipped at small family altars in the house). Some clan halls have recently been restored. You can explore the New Territories by taking the Kowloon–Canton Railway from Hunghom railway station and getting off at any of the stations; or explore on the local buses, or take a six-hour 'Land Between' tour, organised by the Hong Kong Tourist Association for about HK$220 (tel. 5244191).

WHAT TO SEE

◆◆◆
CASTLE PEAK

The sheltered Castle Peak Bay was used in the 11th century as a lay-by port for all manner of trading boats from the Indian Ocean and the Middle East. Here boats converged, awaiting the arrival of monsoon winds to assist their passage to Canton. The bay gradually silted up and is just a swimming beach today.

Castle Peak Monastery overlooks Tuen Mun New Town and Castle Peak Bay from the slope of 2,000-ft (600m) high Ching Shan (Green Mountain, as it is called in Chinese, but Castle Peak in English). It is believed to have been established more than 1,500 years ago by a roving Buddhist monk called Pei Tu who, it is said, could cross rivers in a wooden bowl. There are many extraordinary tales about the monastery's founder. The monastery must have been quite important to Chinese

Junks come to rest in the tranquil Castle Peak Bay

seamen, whose boats used to gather in the bay, but the present buildings date from the 1920s only. The terraced halls of the monastery are surrounded by pine trees, fruit trees and gardens, and the graves of its monks and nuns over the ages. Three large gold leaf, wooden statues—the Buddhas of the Past, Present and Future—stand encased in the main hall. A small stone statue of the Founder

stands in a cave alcove above the monastery, where he is said to have spent time in meditation. It is thought that the statue may have been carved as early as AD954.

Although it is a Buddhist establishment, the architecture and some of the statuary are Taoist additions, for during most of the 19th century it was, in fact, a Taoist temple. A small vegetarian restaurant serves visitors and devotees. The monastery is the oldest in the territory.

Ching Chung Koon (Green Pine) Temple on Castle Peak Road is dedicated to one of the Taoist Eight Immortals, Lui Tung Bun, expeller of evil. He fulfils his task with the aid of a magical fly-switch and sword. The temple is a centre of Taoist studies with a very valuable library of almost 4,000 volumes and some fine works of art. A 1,000-year-old jade seal, imperial palace lanterns and antique porcelain adorn the halls. The buildings themselves are not old—not much more than

20 years—but the hall interiors are ornate and traditional. Apart from scholarly pursuits, the temple supports an old people's home within the complex. It is popular among locals who like to visit the temple, bonzai shrubs and large garden, and eat at its vegetarian restaurant.

Dragon Pottery Kiln, near the 19½ mile-stone of Castle Peak Road, is a rare example of an ancient form of Chinese pottery kiln construction, although this one was probably built in the 1940s. The brick, wood-fired kiln is some 65ft (20m) in length and ascends the hillside, looking for all the world like a dragon. Until very recently the kiln was fired regularly, producing everyday pottery plates, flower pots and cooking ware. There are plans to convert the kiln into a pottery museum.

FANLING
The morning (10.30 to 12 noon) **Luen Wo Market**, off Sha Tau Kok Road at Fanling, is a typical New Territories market place, where arithmetic is done on an abacus and the smells of beancurd, ginger, garlic and fish pervade. There are two fine old walled villages around Fanling: **San Wai** was settled by the Tang Clan about 250 years ago and some 30-odd families live in the village, some still bearing the Tang name. The dry moat still exists but all that remains of the walls is the main gate tower with a superb old iron lattice gate. The walled village of **Hakka Wai** is a beautiful example of Chinese village architecture. It was built in 1905 by the Wong family and the villagers are very proud of it. Terracotta frogs and fishes decorate the roof drains and a three-storey watch tower stands at one end of the village.

SAI KUNG PENINSULA
This area of the New Territories is the most beautiful and certainly, to date, least developed region, with lovely mountains, valleys, old villages and stretches of beach. Marinas and yacht clubs are a feature of Hebe Haven, and there are waterfront restaurants and an old market place at Sai Kung town. Several temples and shrines in Sai Kung are dedicated to Tin Hau, Goddess of the Sea, and to Koon Yum, Goddess of Mercy, and annual festivals are big events for the fishing communities in Port Shelter and Rocky Harbour.

The tiny agricultural village of **Sheung Yiu**, Hebe Haven, has been converted to a museum of folk tradition, with exhibits of farm tools, cooking utensils and household furnishings (open daily 09.00–16.00; closed Tuesdays).

Lei Yue Mun Village, at the edge of Kowloon, is a fishing village, famous for its seaside restaurants. The seafood vendors keep their live produce in gurgling tanks and vats, and each evening the main village alley livens up as Cantonese seafood gourmets descend, often from pleasure craft. They bargain fiercely, then carry their purchases off to a favourite nearby restaurant to be cooked. Be warned, though, that this is not a cheap way to dine.

SHA TIN

During the Ch'ing dynasty (1644–1911), rice grown in quiet Sha Tin valley was so excellent that it was reserved for the emperor alone. The inlet and gentle green valley gave a peaceful picture even in the early 1970s. Today it is a modern city with a projected population of 700,000 by the mid-1990s!

Amah's Rock above Sha Tin, watches over these giant changes. The rock, in the shape of a woman carrying a child on her back, has a moving legend attached to it. It is said that the woman is the wife of a bodyguard of the last Sung boy-emperor, who was killed in

Hong Kong is not all skyscrapers: this Chinese village is in Sha Tin

battle. Each evening she would carry her child to the peak and wait in vain for her husband. Eventually the gods took pity on her and turned her body to stone while releasing her soul to be united with her husband.

Che Kung Temple, Che Kung Miu Road, is dedicated to a Sung dynasty (960–1270) general, whose military exploits earned deification after his death. The temple was erected, around 1825, in his honour after a villager dreamt that the god had stopped a deadly plague which ravaged the village towards the end of the Ming dynasty. On the third day of each lunar New Year the Che Kung festival draws tens of thousands of worshippers. On the altar is a wheel which symbolises the cosmic rotation of the year. Devotees turn this to bring good luck for the new year and present their offerings. Che Kung is especially popular amongst gamblers! Che Kung Temple is a 10-minute walk from the KCR Tai Wai railway station.

The Chinese University campus on Tai Po Road at Sha Tin was established in 1963 and courses are taught principally in Chinese, but English is also a teaching medium. Competition is very keen for the 7,000 or so places. An extra-mural department has an enrolment of some 56,000 students. The University offers degree courses in arts, business administration, science, social science and medicine, and has its own **art gallery** in which exhibitions are held regularly. The University's own collection includes ancient bronze seals, jade flower carvings, paintings and

A golden Buddha dwarfs the ranks of nearly 13,000 tiny statues in Ten Thousand Buddhas Monastery

calligraphy (open daily, 10.00–16.30; Sundays and public holidays 12.30–16.30).
KCR: University station.

Tao Fong Shan is a hill to the northwest of Sha Tin where the Chinese Mission to Buddhists has stood since 1931. The founder was Karl Ludwig Reichelt, whose life was

in 1950. The walls of the main hall are lined with 12,800 tiny statues and three large gilded ones of the Lord Buddha. Three other small temples make up the complex, one of which has the embalmed body of the founder monk, Yuet Kai, who died in 1965 at the grand old age of 87. It is said that his body was found to be in perfect condition when, following the monks' instructions, it was exhumed eight months later. The miraculous body was lacquered and encased in gold leaf and, before a congregation of 10,000 Buddhists, was enthroned at the foot of the huge 40-ft (12m) high Buddha in the temple. A climb to the top of the pink pagoda affords a panoramic view of Sha Tin below.

Half an hour's walk from KCR Sha Tin station.

Sha Tin Race Course was opened in 1978 and stands on 250 acres of reclaimed land. Its facilities, which include air-conditioned stables, are among the most modern in the world, and its spectator stands accommodate 70,000 racing enthusiasts (see **Sporting Activities**, page 109).

KCR Race Course station.

Tsang Tai Uk (Tsang's Big House), near Tai Chung Kui Road and Sha Kok Street, was built as the Tsang clan family residence in the 1840s. It has a high rectangular defensive wall and corner towers with *wok-yee* (meaning 'ear of a cooking pan') roofs. Atop each corner tower is a trident to ward off evil. The dwellings within face on to a central courtyard; two wells provided its water. One local legend says that the family's

dedicated to teaching Christianity to Buddhists. The buildings integrate Buddhist architectural principles and the gardens are wonderfully peaceful. Former monks are engaged in painting pottery as a means of contributing to the mission.

Half an hour's walk from KCR Sha Tin station.

Five hundred steps lead to the hilltop **Ten Thousand Buddhas Monastery (Man Fat Sze)**, built

Hong Kong's second race course, at Sha Tin, took seven years to build

prosperity was due to the visitation of pirates, who left several large jars of fish in the safe-keeping of the Tsang clan headman. When the pirates failed to return, the fish were thrown away and, behold, the pots were full of silver coins. The Tsangs then decided to build their fortified village to defend themselves against the return of the pirates. It is said the village took 20 years to construct. Many of the houses are rented out and only a few members of the Tsang family reside there now. Tsang Tai Uk is a 15-minute walk from the KCR Tai Wai railway station.

◆
SHEUNG SHUI
Sheung Shui is the last stop on the KCR railway if you are not bound for China. Hakka women with their distinctive black fringed hats are frequent shoppers in the covered market in the centre of the old section of town. The market played a vital rôle in Sheung Shui; regular market days were the economic focus of the town until the 1940s. From **Lok Ma Chau Lookout** the view sweeps across duck and fish ponds to beyond the Hong Kong/China border river of Shenzhen into mainland China. A major border crossing point is under construction near by.

TAI PO

The old Tai Po market town has been transformed by massive reclamation along the seashore of Tolo Harbour where residential blocks and an industrial estate have been constructed. Tai Po's market is still of interest, as is the white colonial style bungalow known as **Island House**, on Tai Po Road, now occupied by the World Wide Fund for Nature but formerly the home of successive Tai Po district officers. Island House was used as the Japanese command headquarters for the New Territories during World War II.

The old railway station building at Tai Po has been turned into the **Kowloon–Canton Railway Museum** with old carriages and memorabilia of its heyday (open daily, except Tuesdays, 09.00–16.00).

From Ma Lin Shui pier a ferry leaves twice a day on a four-hour round trip to islands in Tolo Harbour. As early as the 8th century, historical records mention pearl diving in Tolo Harbour by Tanka people as corvée labour. Divers were weighted down with stones and were pulled to the surface by a rope when on the point of suffocation. Surprisingly, the Mongol Yuan Dynasty considered it inhumane and in the 14th century prohibited the industry. But it seems to have resumed again in the Ming dynasty (1368–1644). For information on this trip contact the Hong Kong Tourist Association (see **Tourist Advice**, page 123).

Kadoorie Experimental Farm, on Lam Kam Road to the west of Tai Po along the Lam Tsuen Valley, is a beautiful garden of trees, shrubs and flowers. It forms part of a 360-acre farm run by the two Kadoorie brothers, well known Hong Kong philanthropists. Since 1949 their Agricultural Aid Association has given aid and know-how in agriculture and animal husbandry, built roads and bridges, and helped more than 1,200 villages in the territory. A re-training programme has also been established for Gurkha soldiers returning to their villages in Nepal. Visits to the farm can be arranged—they are by appointment only (tel. 4881317).

On the north side of Tolo Harbour lies Plover Cove Reservoir, above which is the beautiful Pak Sin Range, offering hard but rewarding walks. The road leads on towards Starling Inlet via **Bride's Pool**, where a small waterfall makes a popular picnic spot.

At **Luk Keng** an egretry has been established for the small egrets which nest here during the summer months. The low mangroves and still water make ideal fishing grounds for the birds. As many as 800 nests have been counted among the forest of trees on the small hill. The road links up with the Sha Tau Kok Road. The town of Sha Tau Kok (within the closed border area) can be seen across the inlet. This is a town which has been transformed in recent years from a tiny border village to an important border crossing town.

◆◆
YUEN LONG

Concentrated urbanisation has taken place in Yuen Long, with major public and private housing projects. This once sleepy market town now has a population of around 86,500 and by 1995 this should reach 161,000. Yuen Long is linked to Tuen Mun by a light rail system which opened in 1988.

East of Yuen Long lie the 500-year-old walled villages of the Tang clan, the most accessible being **Kat Hing Wai**, better known as **Kam Tin Village**, on Kam Tin Road. The walls and corner towers were built to defend villages against pirate incursion and the rich Tang clan were obvious targets. In 1898 the British army took retribution against the Tang, who were militant towards the British takeover of the New Territories, by removing their handsome iron gates. After adorning an Irish garden for 26 years the gates were returned to the village in 1925. This is the most commercialised of the New Territories villages and is geared for tourists.

Lau Fau Shan, a fishing village to the west of Yuen Long, is famous for its seafood restaurants. The narrow main street is lined with vendors selling dried seafood specialities and live fish, prawns, crabs, whelks, and oysters from aerated tanks. You may buy what you fancy and take it to any restaurant in the village for cooking. (The fresh sweet egg rolls made here are very good, too.) The morning fish market, which supplies fish and shellfish to most of the New Territories and Kowloon restaurants, is very lively and competitive. Most of the villagers make their living from oyster beds in Deep Bay, but recently these have suffered from pollution. Oyster shells bank the shorefront.

Ha Tsuen Village, near by, built by the Tang clan, has a fine 18th-century ancestral hall. Inside its grey brick walls are two courtyards, and the main hall has

two wooden tablets with the characters for brotherly love and filial piety. The ancestral tablets are arranged on an ornately carved altar. Just inside the entrance is a 'spirit wall' which traditionally prevents ghosts and evil spirits from entering the hall. A 19th-century Chinese cannon, unearthed near the village in 1979, stands at the doorway. Outside **Ping Shan Village** stands an elegant 200-year-old three-storey brick pagoda, the Tsui Shing Lau. The pagoda is said to have originally had seven storeys, but these appear to have been lost in typhoons. It is simple and graceful and this pagoda is also the only old one left in the territory.

For those who think of Hong Kong as crowds and skyscrapers, areas such as these New Territories rice fields can be a revelation

A pied kingfisher – one of the hundreds of species of birds to be seen at Mai Po Marshes

Mai Po Marshes Bird Sanctuary

Mai Po Marshes Bird Sanctuary, on the Hong Kong-Chinese border, off Castle Peak Road, between Fanling and Yuen Long, is a designated World Wide Fund for Nature wetlands. Over 250 species of birds have been sighted during the migratory season when Mai Po's ponds, mudflats and mangroves serve as a vital feeding site. Commonly seen are herons, egrets, kingfishers and ibises. There are well-constructed hides and a boardwalk which gives access to the mangrove swamps. The Chinese Government has also declared 7 miles (11km) of contiguous wetlands a nature reserve, and it is hoped that further developmental encroachment can be contained. A visit here, however, requires some forethought, as the area is near the border and is restricted. An entry permit must be obtained from the Agriculture and Fisheries Dept, Canton Road Government Offices, 393 Canton Road, Kowloon.

San Tin Village on Castle Peak Road near the Mai Po Marshes is an extended village founded by the Man clan and has at least five large ancestral halls. The oldest, built in the late 17th century, has three halls with decorated and carved wooden roof supports and stone columns. Although it has not been restored recently it is still in reasonable, if dusty, condition. The ancestral tablets are arrayed on a central altar. The newest hall was built in 1972 and is an interesting contrast in style and taste. In 1865 a successful Man clan member who achieved high honours in the Imperial Civil Service examinations in Peking, built himself a grand two-storey family residence in grey brick, known as Tai Fu Tai. The house has recently been beautifully restored with financial assistance from the Hong Kong Jockey Club. Its wooden carvings and wall paintings have been repaired and repainted, and ancestral portraits hung above the altar. The tiled roof is adorned with brightly glazed terracotta figures and a large side-kitchen shows a complex series of cooking stoves. Behind the house is a grove of shady, old *lichee* (lychee) trees.

OUTLYING ISLANDS

There are 235 islands in Hong Kong waters. Most of them are barren rocks with no water supply and therefore uninhabitable; others have small fishing communities. A ferry ride and half-day or day's exploration of one or more of these islands is an opportunity to enjoy the slower pace of village life, or to walk their peaceful hills for stunning sea views.

Ferries for the main islands leave from the Outlying Islands District Services Pier west of the Star Ferry on Hong Kong Island.

About 10 per cent of Cheung Chau's population lives in the 'junk villages' off the island's shores

Check the ferry schedule either with the Hong Kong & Yau Ma Tei Ferry Co (tel. 5423081) or with the Hong Kong Tourist Association (tel. 7225555). It is preferable to go on a weekday, as the weekend ferries are packed with young holiday-makers. Ferry fares range from HK$4 to $12. Detailed maps of the islands can be purchased at the Government Publications Office, General Post Office Building, beside the Hong Kong Star Ferry concourse.

◆◆◆
CHEUNG CHAU

The small island of Cheung Chau, a 45-minute ferry ride from Central, has become a commuter island, as rents are

Beaches and an absence of traffic draw visitors to Cheung Chau

low and the ferry service frequent. The population is now 40,000 but it retains much character with a busy market and harbour, temples, beaches and scenic walks. Cars are not allowed on the island. A hundred years ago Cheung Chau was the home of a pirate fleet of over 250 junks. On the southern tip of the island is the **Cheung Po Tsai Cave**, named after their commander. Even as recently as the 1920s, pirates would harass passing boats. There are a number of temples on the island, but the most important is **Pak Tai Temple**, in whose honour the spectacular Bun Festival is held annually. On the east side of the island, along Hak Pak Road on the beachfront, are ancient rock carvings depicting animal shapes which may have been carved two or three thousand years ago. Shops sell paper houses, cars, clothing, etc, for burning at funerals, for Cheung Chau is considered geomantically very auspicious for burials, and there are many cemeteries on the southern part of the island.

LAMMA

Ferries link the two main villages of **Yung Shue Wan** and **Sok Kwu Wan** on Lamma Island with Central, and a *kai do* (motorised sampan) service operates between Aberdeen and Sok Kwu Wan. The island's population of only 5,000 are either vegetable growers or run fish farms in the bays, but there are 'city' types, too, who commute every day. Carbon dating of archaeological finds indicates that Lamma was occupied as early as 4000BC. A favourite walk over the hills between the two main villages of Yung Shue Wan and Sok Kwu Wan takes less than two hours. The open-air seafood restaurants at Sok Kwu Wan are very popular, especially at night.

◆◆◆
LANTAU

Lantau is a beautiful island of mountains, valleys, beaches, peaceful monasteries, and old Chinese forts, which is twice the size of Hong Kong Island but with a population of less than 20,000. It is ideal for walking and there are two designated country parks with well marked hiking paths. At Discovery Bay a large residential scheme offers sporting facilities, including a golf course, and a fast boat service operates from Blake Pier in Central to the bay for commuters and visitors alike. The Lantau ferry (which takes just over an hour) docks at Silvermine Bay. Buses leave from the ferry pier for the villages of Tai O and Tung Chung and for Po Lin Monastery. There is a taxi service but hire cars need to be arranged beforehand with the Lantau Tour Company (tel. 9848255/6). Several richly endowed neolithic and Bronze Age archaeological sites have been excavated on Lantau, indicating that the island was occupied as early as 2500BC. At the end of the 13th century the exiled court of the last Sung Dynasty child emperor resided for a short time on Lantau.

Cheung Sha is a long sandy beach, the best on the island, just beyond Pui O on the southern coast of the island; and **Mui Wo** is a small beachfront resort with a market and seafood restaurants situated in Silvermine Bay.

Po Lin Monastery (Precious Lotus Monastery) was founded in 1905, and stands on Lantau Peak, 2,460ft (750m) above sea level. Buddhist monks from other parts of southeast Asia gather here every two years for meditation and special initiation ceremonies. The present buildings were built in 1970 and the temple architecture is on a grand scale, with marble terraces and striking yellow roof tiles. It is dedicated to the Three Precious Buddhas – the religion's founder, Lord Sakyamuni, the Healing Buddha, and Lord of the Western Paradise, Amitabha. A vegetarian restaurant serves simple meals to the thousands of weekly visitors and the income from this enterprise and from donations supports the monastery. A 250-tonne bronze statue of the Buddha is being cast, at a cost of HK$68 million, for the monastery in China, and when *in situ* will be the tallest in southeast Asia. Visitors may stay overnight at the monastery and climb the 3,000-ft (934m) high Lantau Peak to watch the sunrise. Close by is a tea plantation growing 'cloud and mist tea', which can be tasted in its gardens.

Tai O village has a population of 2,000, who are mostly engaged in catching and drying fish. Dried out salt pans are all that remains of the salt factories which flourished here 200 years ago. It is a quaint village, with many fishing huts built on stilts along the tidal creek, which is crossed in a rope-drawn sampan (a 20 cent ride). The narrow Market Street leads to the 18th-century **Kwan Tai Temple**, and to the 17th-century **Hau Wong Temple**. A festival is held each year to commemorate Hau Wong, who was the Marquis Yang Liang Chieh, a beloved guardian of the last Sung dynasty boy-emperor.

Tung Chung Village is the site of a Chinese fort built in 1817 by the Viceroy of Kwangtung; its cannon served to repel coastal attacks. It has thick granite stone walls and ramparts which display six Chinese cannon, the

earliest dated 1805. The fort has been restored as a historical monument. On the bluff overlooking the ferry pier and bay are the ruins of the Tung Chung Battery. Local Chinese historical records refer to it as forming a part of the coastal fortification, but the site has not been excavated. The village also has a Hau Wong Temple.

PENG CHAU

Ferries bound for Lantau Island normally stop *en route* at Peng Chau pier. The residents here are mostly engaged in fishing or fish farming, though there are some porcelain factories in operation. The island does not offer much in the way of beaches or pleasant walks, beyond the curiosity of exploration.

The dazzlingly decorated Po Lin Monastery on Lantau Island

PEACE AND QUIET:

Wildlife and Countryside in Hong Kong

Although many of the territory's animals and plants are widespread throughout the mainland of China, Hong Kong provides the easiest opportunities to see them. It is also on an important migration route for birds heading from their Asian breeding grounds to winter in the tropics, and its coastal marshes, in particular, are of international importance. Hong Kong has a wide variety of habitats and its scenery is often dramatic. Beaches, mangroves, marshes and cliffs line undeveloped stretches of the coast and rise inland to hills and mountains nearly 3,000 ft (1,000m) above sea level. In places, woodlands and open grassland cover these heights and upland valleys sometimes also contain reservoirs.

The variety of habitats is reflected in the wealth of plant and animal species found; for example, nearly 400 species of birds have been recorded, over 100 of which breed. Butterflies are diverse and abundant and there are nearly 2,500 species of native and introduced flowering plants and ferns.

Land of Contrasts

First impressions would perhaps lead the visitor to suppose that this is not an area for the wildlife enthusiast. While this may be true of many of the more built up areas, places of tranquil beauty can be found without too much difficulty, with colourful and exotic butterflies and birds. Despite its well-deserved reputation for being overcrowded, Hong Kong's densely-packed urban areas are comparatively restricted and over three-quarters of the 400 or so square miles (1,000 sq km) in the territory can be classed as countryside. While much of the land is in some way influenced by man or his agriculture, 21 country parks, covering an area of 100,000 acres, have been established and a further series of nature reserves helps conserve the land and its wildlife. The parks and reserves cover all types of habitat from the coastal beaches and marshes to wooded hills and reservoirs, and in addition to the birds and flowering plants, mammals such as barking deer, porcupine and civet also benefit from this protection.

On Hong Kong Island itself, the Botanical Gardens in the Central District have been established since 1871 and their quiet corners are attractive to both resident and wintering birds. Elsewhere, there are five country parks and the 30-mile (50km) 'Hong Kong Trail' has been set out to enable the hiker to traverse them all. Particularly interesting is the Aberdeen Country Park, which lies inland from Deep Water Bay, and has extensive woodlands which enclose two reservoirs. Spotted doves, black-throated laughing doves, light-vented bulbuls, greater coucals and Chinese blue magpies are all regularly seen from the nature trail which winds through the park, and singing insects serenade the visitor from the foliage.

At least one of Hong Kong's birds

PEACE AND QUIET

actually seems to benefit from the abundance of people. Black kites, often referred to as black-eared kites, are abundant and thrive on refuse. On an environmental level, sewage and litter, animal waste and industrial emissions are a real problem for the Hong Kong authorities, but fortunately, the problem is now recognised and immediate and long-term plans to curb and monitor pollution are having a real effect.

Boat Trips

In a territory where many of the people live on offshore islands, boats are an essential mode of transport. There are also many sight-seeing trips available and together with the ferries they provide an extremely pleasant way of seeing Hong Kong and visiting the more distant peninsulas and remote islands. Some of the journeys are comparatively short and may simply involve crossing a harbour, while others, such as the ferry to Lantau, are much longer. After a while, long sea journeys can become a little monotonous, so what better way to inject interest than to observe the wildlife?

In shallow bays and unpolluted harbours you may see shoals of fish. The marine life in the South China Sea off Hong Kong is exceedingly rich and diverse and this is especially evident in the numbers of fish. About 1,500 species are found in the inshore waters, coral reefs and open seas around the coast, this wealth being manifested in the extraordinary variety found in the markets of Hong Kong.

Cattle egrets are usually to be found on cultivated land and in marshy areas such as Mai Po

The secret of the diversity of Hong Kong's marine environment lies in its position on the Asian coast. The warm, tropical waters bathing coastlines further south are continually tempered by the cold, nutrient-rich Hainan current which sweeps down from the north past Japan. The balance of cool and warm water varies according to season but the continued input of nutrients

months, black-headed gulls, and, to a lesser extent, herring and yellow-legged gulls linger around the harbours, but further offshore the only species likely to be seen are stray pelagic seabirds. Sooty and bridled terns and occasionally even a frigatebird occur, especially shortly after a typhoon or tropical storm.

Mai Po Marshes

Mai Po Marshes offer some of the best birdwatching in Hong Kong. A patchwork of mangroves and brackish and tidal pools attracts vast numbers of water birds including waders, herons, egrets, terns and kingfishers. Not only are the numbers of birds impressive, but the variety is also outstanding. Over 250 species have been recorded, some of which are year-round residents while others are passage migrants or winter visitors.

Most of Mai Po is enclosed within the boundaries of an official nature reserve, managed by the World Wide Fund for Nature (Hong Kong). In order to visit the reserve, permits are needed and must be applied for in advance from the Director of Agriculture and Fisheries; but the effort required to obtain one will be well rewarded.

As an alternative, it is sometimes possible to join one of the Hong Kong Birdwatching Society's regular visits; but failing this, the ponds adjacent to the road from Mai Po village to the reserve entrance are still rich in birdlife. Visitors should always bear in mind the proximity of the border with the People's Republic of

ensures that a healthy food chain is perpetuated.

Man is not the only mammal to exploit the harvest of the sea around Hong Kong, and, well away from the shore, large species of whale are occasionally seen. Closer to land, Chinese white dolphins and bottle-nosed dolphins sometimes bow-ride the boats, maintaining impressive bursts of speed.

More remote coasts and bays have ospreys or white-bellied sea-eagles, but neither stray far from land. During the winter

PEACE AND QUIET

Great egrets are the largest marsh birds of the region

China and respect instructions from the police, who are ever-alert for illegal immigrants. Throughout the year, the pools are thronged with Chinese pond-herons, little and great egrets, while ever-present are the black kites which scavenge any scraps from left-over meals. Common sandpipers wade in the shallow mud in search of invertebrates, and in the mangroves, white-breasted and common kingfishers perch on the look-out for fish below. Crested bulbuls, black-faced laughing-thrushes and white-eyes feed among the foliage of bushes. Magpie-robins, with their conspicuous black-and-white plumage, prefer more open areas.

From October to March, wintering birds such as bluethroat, wryneck, and Richard's pipit feed around the dry, muddy margins to the pools. Waders, too, spend the winter here and in Deep Bay, but during migration time, their numbers and varieties increase dramatically, and it is not uncommon to see over 30 species in a single day. Grey-rumped sandpiper, whimbrel, red-necked stint, great knot and terek sandpiper wade in the shallow water while overhead, Caspian, gull-billed and whiskered terns hover and plunge-dive.

Deep Bay

Deep Bay, in the far northwest of the New Territories, is one of Hong Kong's best birdwatching spots. Although the area may lack a little of the variety offered by the Mai Po Nature Reserve which it adjoins, it has the great advantage of being far more accessible. From the shoreline, on which some of the birds roost at high-tide, vast mudflats stretch away into the distance when the tide is out and provide a rich feeding ground for waders, ducks, terns and gulls.

In common with Mai Po, Deep Bay is especially good during spring and autumn migration time and many of the birds commute between the two sites. Up to 40 species of wader can be recorded in a single season, some of them being difficult to see anywhere else in the world, and fabled names like Nordmann's greenshank and spoon-billed sandpiper lure many migrant birdwatchers to stop off in Hong Kong on long-haul flights.

Deep Bay at low-tide presents a vast area of organically-rich mud on which the feeding birds are evenly spread, and consequently most are extremely distant. However, as the tide rises, they are pushed closer and closer to the shore and then provide much better views. To see the mudflats at their best, the stretch of coast between Lau Fau Shan and Tsim Bei Tsui is best and, beyond this point, visitors can continue on foot to within sight of Mai Po. During the winter, by scanning the bay at high tide or deep water channels at low tide,

great-crested grebes, cormorants, red-breasted mergansers and even Dalmatian pelicans may be seen. Although regularly seen here, this last species is rare on a global scale and considered endangered. Pied kingfishers occasionally hover and plunge into the water after fish but are more regularly seen perched around coastal pools.

Teal, wigeon, shelduck and other dabbling duck prefer to feed on organisms in the exposed mud and are more easily seen at low tide. Black-headed gulls can be numerous and feed either by paddling the mud to disturb hidden animals or sometimes by coercing other birds into giving up their own meals. They are by far the commonest gull in the region—almost all are winter visitors—but they are sometimes joined by larger herring and yellow-legged gulls.

Waders in Deep Bay

Although rich in all forms of water-loving birds, the mudflats of Deep Bay are especially renowned for the numbers and variety of waders that they support. Casual observers cannot fail to be impressed by the sight and sound of the huge winter flocks, and hardened enthusiasts, keen to identify the maximum number of species, and hopefully a few rarities, are seldom disappointed. Since most of the waders are either passage migrants, passing through in spring and autumn, or winter visitors from August until April, there is something of interest throughout the year.

PEACE AND QUIET

Although to many people waders tend to look rather similar, many of those that occur in Deep Bay are either well-marked or comparatively large and easily identified. Whimbrels and curlews with their long, down-curved beaks are not easily mistaken and black-tailed and bar-tailed godwits are recognised by their long, slightly up-curved beaks.

Smaller waders are also well represented and Kentish plovers and greater sand-plovers are numerous. Curlew sandpipers, easily picked out in flight by their white rumps, are also common, along with red-necked stints, but at least 10 potentially confusing species also occur regularly, so careful observations are necessary. Many of these birds have rather specialised beaks which have evolved to suit their method of feeding. Perhaps most bizarre is the tiny spoon-billed sandpiper whose spatulate-tipped bill helps filter minute organisms from the mud. Terek sandpipers are also fascinating to watch as they chase along with their long, up-turned bills flicking from side to side. Their bright yellow legs are set so far back on their bodies that they give the impression that if they stopped moving they would fall over. Spotted redshanks are common passage migrants to Deep Bay, their loud 'kewick' call being distinctive. They are sometimes joined by redshank and greenshank, but pride of place must go to Nordmann's greenshank, a handful of which are seen each year. This bird can be distinguished from the more frequent greenshank by its yellow legs, yellow base to the bill and webbed toes. Although identification requires patient observation, success means a real blue-riband day for the birdwatcher.

Mangroves
Throughout the tropical regions of the world, river estuaries, mudflats and quiet backwaters support extraordinary swamp forests of mangrove. These evergreen trees are among the few plants capable of growing in the harsh conditions of choking silt and salty water and are so well-adapted to this environment that they are vital to the stabilisation of the mud and the creation of new land. Around the shores of Hong Kong, the mangroves are now much reduced due to the activities of man, but they can still be seen in places around Deep Bay and Mai Po.

Of the 30 or so species of mangrove which grow around the coasts of the South China Sea, each one is best suited to a different position on the shore according to the amount of salt or freshwater and the exposure to air at low tide which it can tolerate. The tangled network of roots, so characteristic of this habitat, serves to anchor the plants in the shifting mud, and aerial roots facilitate gas exchange otherwise impossible in the sticky mud. The roots inadvertently trap more and more silt and are forced to extend higher and higher, and over a period of decades, this gradually consolidates the mud to form dry land.

The roots provide a haven for many species of fish and crab. The curious mudskipper fish, capable of hopping around on bare mud, and fiddler crabs, the males with their brightly

A few areas of mangrove swamp persist around the coast

coloured pincers, dot the surface. The mangroves are also a safe nursery for young fish which, when full-grown, are open water species. Many of these are important commercial fish later in life and to destroy mangrove swamps not only wrecks a fascinating

PEACE AND QUIET

environment but also seriously affects the future prospects of many fisheries.

Mangroves also harbour a variety of birds; white-eyes forage among the foliage while, on the mud below, waders such as Kentish plover and red-necked stint feast on the invertebrate life found there. White-breasted kingfishers perch in the branches and dive down to capture fish and crabs, even when the water level is surprisingly low. By day, great and little egrets stalk patiently through the channels of water, while after dark they are replaced by night herons.

Tai Po Kau Nature Reserve

Lying above Tolo Harbour, Tai Po Kau Nature Reserve holds what is probably the best example of native woodland left in Hong Kong. Popular as a beauty spot with both residents and tourists, the rolling countryside is scenically attractive and the natural forests harbour a wealth of interesting plants and animals. In particular, the birdwatching within the reserve is excellent both for resident species and migrants, many of which are seldom recorded elsewhere in Hong Kong.

As with many other sites in Hong Kong, disturbance caused by people at weekends and on public holidays can make birdwatching difficult, especially in the vicinity of the car parks and picnic sites. However, a nature trail and several forest walks, coloured-coded according to distance, allow those with a more serious interest to escape the noise and clamour.

Birdwatching in Tai Po Kau is good throughout the year but during migration, from March to May and August to October, the rewards may be unexpected and all the more exciting: after a short period of bad weather, the bushes can be alive with birds. Brown, blue-and-white and Asian paradise flycatchers may be among them, males of the last species being a particularly beautiful sight with their long, chestnut tails.

From October to March, the forests play host to a range of winter visitors. Red-throated, olive-backed and Richard's pipits feed in the open areas or along the trails, sometimes in the company of pale and grey-backed thrushes. Mixed parties of warblers, flycatchers and other small passerines are also present. They move around a lot and can be difficult to see, but with patience, perseverance and a good ear, the visitor is likely to encounter a flock.

Although many of Tai Po Kau's resident birds are shy and retiring, this is by no means true of all of them. Great barbets, with their green and chestnut plumage and yellow beaks, sometimes sit on bare branches, while black drongos draw attention to themselves with their hissing call and habit of perching in the open. Colourful Chinese blue (or red-billed) magpies are occasionally seen among the foliage, and resident scarlet minivets and treepies are also conspicuous, numbers of the latter two species being swollen in the winter by migrants.

The Chinese blue magpie is perhaps one of Hong Kong's most attractive birds

Sai Kung Country Park

Set in the extreme east of the New Territories, the scenery of the Sai Kung Peninsula is among the finest in Hong Kong. Despite the creation of the High Island Reservoir within the boundaries of the Country Park, most of the park's landscape has probably changed little in centuries. Natural woodlands and scrub merge with grassland and plantations and, here and there, the remains of long-abandoned villages and temples add cultural interest.

Sai Kung can be reached from Hong Kong Island either on the coast road which runs to Tai Mong Tsai or by ferry. These run on a daily basis, but for more adventurous visitors, youth hostels and camp sites provide cheap bases from which to explore the park more thoroughly. For long- or medium-distance walks visitors can join the MacLehose Trail which for part of its length runs through the park. The trek eventually leads west away from Sai Kung and winds for 60 miles (100km) across eight country parks and through some wonderful scenery until it reaches Tuen Mun.

PEACE AND QUIET

Among the scrub and open woodland, the visitor will hear the grating call of the Chinese francolin. These partridge-like gamebirds often call from the open in spring but for the rest of the year are rather wary. This is not surprising, since they are frequently caught and can be found in most of Hong Kong's markets.

In spring and autumn, hundreds of tired migrant birds, including dollarbirds and flycatchers, pass through the park and mixed flocks of small passerines feed in the bushes. They join common resident birds such as greater coucal, great tit and white-eye, numbers of the latter species

Parks and gardens are favoured habitats for the red-whiskered bulbul, a boldly marked bird

being boosted in winter by birds from the mainland. Chinese, red-vented and crested (red-whiskered) bulbuls are often seen, sometimes in quite large flocks. During the breeding season, however, the males are territorial and crested bulbuls in particular advertise their presence with a loud song.

On warm days, butterflies dance through the open woodland and lizards and snakes bask in the sun's rays. Fortunately for those with an aversion to snakes, most species are generally timid and retreat if disturbed. However, do not ever be tempted to try to handle one because at least eight of Hong Kong's species are highly venomous; these include the banded krait, the King cobra and the bamboo snake.

Lion Rock Country Park

Across the waters of Victoria Harbour, the Lion Rock Country Park is one of the first areas of countryside reached on leaving Hong Kong Island for the New Territories. The hill country which comprises the park's 1,300 acres is dominated by Lion Rock itself, an outcrop of granite that, from some angles, resembles a crouched lion. Although decades of interference by man have reduced the park's woodland to a sorry state, a programme of intensive planting and conservation work is now underway to restore the natural cover.

Lion Rock has always been a popular destination for local residents and tourists alike. Outcrops such as Lion Rock, Mong Fu Shek and Beacon Hill provide wonderful views, but part of the park's attraction must lie in its comparative inaccessibility. Since no public roads run through the park, the only way in is on foot; fortunately there is no shortage of footpaths, some of which form part of the long-distance MacLehose Trail. Replanting of the woodlands has met with mixed success because fires and former land-use had already seriously impoverished the soil. However, Chinese red pine, strawberry tree and ivy tree are common and in the western half of the park, the planting has been deliberately varied to increase its value to wildlife. This is now a designated conservation area and a nature trail allows easy access.

In the wilder regions of the park, swallowtail butterflies flit along the paths while cicadas sing during spring and summer but are infuriatingly difficult to spot. Small parties of ring-necked (or rose-ringed) parakeets screech noisily through the scrub and occasionally breed where the trees are old enough and large enough to provide nesting holes. There is doubt as to whether the parakeets spread naturally to Hong Kong or were introduced to the colony, but whatever the case, they are now quite widespread.

The ubiquitous black kite is also common in the park, its whistling call and forked tail in flight making identification easy. They sometimes nest in the larger pines and their numbers demonstrate how this scavenging bird has profited from man's presence. Also benefiting from human company are the park's long-tailed macaques which, like those around Kowloon reservoir, have learned to accept food from tourists.

Kam Shan Country Park
To the north of Kowloon in the New Territories, the boundaries of Kam Shan Country Park enclose over 740 acres of scrub and semi-natural woodland with much of the land comprising the catchment area for four reservoirs. This hilly park is dominated by the 980-ft (300m) Golden Hill and from here panoramic views can be had of Smuggler's Ridge, Lion Rock, Tai Mo Shan and distant towns and harbours.

Although only a single public road traverses the park, a whole network of signposted footpaths criss-crosses the countryside, allowing almost complete access to Kam Shan. Some of the paths even form part of the MacLehose Trail, the 60-mile (100km) trek which winds its way across most of the New Territories.

Whether you stroll gently around the shores of the reservoirs or through the open woodland of Chinese red pine and slash pine, you will come across a variety of colourful insects. April and May and October and November are the best months for butterflies, and brightly marked skippers and elegant and fast-flying swallowtails provide a dazzling spectacle. Close to the water, metallic dragonflies and damselflies chase smaller insects for food or each other to mate, during which process they fly around in tandem.

Woodland shrews are sometimes seen scurrying

PEACE AND QUIET

A skipper butterfly – one of Hong Kong's colourful insects

among the fallen leaves, but the most conspicuous mammals found in Kam Shan are the long-tailed (or pig-tailed) macaques. Although genuinely wild individuals are found elsewhere in Hong Kong, those along the wooded Tai Po road are descendants of macaques reintroduced in 1920. Under natural conditions, their omnivorous diet would include everything from fruits and nuts to insects and small mammals. Like other monkeys, however, they are naturally inquisitive, especially with regard to food, and have learned to pester picnickers for scraps, which can cause considerable annoyance. Completed in 1910, Kowloon reservoir was the first to be built in the New Territories. Subsequently three smaller reservoirs, Shek Lei Pui, Reception and Byewash, have been constructed. In addition to their scenic appeal, they are of

interest to the birdwatcher, with migrant waders sometimes feeding around their margins and great-crested grebes and several species of duck being seen regularly on their waters.

Yim Tso Ha Egretry
Lying in the northeast of the New Territories, the Yim Tso Ha egretry is a wonderful spectacle from April until August. Protected since 1969, hundreds of pairs of birds now make their twiggy nests among the bushes, whole trees becoming whitewashed with droppings by the end of the season. Although other egretries exist at Mong Tseng Wai and at Mai Po village, Yim Tso Ha is by far the best and most accessible.

The egretry is reached by taking the Tolo Highway north towards the border and turning right towards Sha Tau Kok, this road eventually running along the northern shore of Starling Inlet. At the southwestern end of the inlet, up to six species of heron and egret breed, including as many as 100 pairs of cattle egrets. During the breeding season these attractive birds are easily recognised by their buff throats and crowns and yellow legs and bills.

A few pairs of great egrets also breed in among the larger numbers of night herons and elegantly-plumed little egrets. The more observant visitors may spot one of the few pairs of the endangered Swinhoe's egret, which breed at Yim Tso Ha. Distinguished by its yellow toes and bill and blue-grey facial skin, this is one of the world's rarest birds.

FOOD AND DRINK

A rich and varied eating adventure can be undertaken in the cornucopia of Hong Kong's restaurants. The cuisines of China, southeast Asia, India, Pakistan, Japan, Korea and Europe are all represented, and standards are high.

Chinese

Whatever the regional cuisine, it aims to maintain a delicate balance between the positive (*yang*) and negative (*ying*) forces of the universe, as advocated by the ancient Taoists. This is created, in Chinese food, by the harmonious ordering of dishes, which should produce the correct healthy

It is worth learning to use chopsticks; some restaurants may offer no alternatives!

balance of cold and hot, bland and spicy, sour and sweet. The dietary principles of Chinese cuisine were established many centuries ago, and though they may appear mere superstition to many young Chinese, they are nevertheless still adhered to. The foods which are said to have aphrodisiac qualities—snake bladder, ginseng and chicken, steamed carp—are very expensive. It is said that eggplant can cause female infertility and pig's brain can cause male impotence. Snake soup with shredded chrysanthemum petals is considered a great winter restorative. Other expensive dishes are eaten for their texture—bird's nests and *bêche-de-mer*—which does not normally appeal to the foreign palate.

FOOD AND DRINK

A Chinese dinner is best enjoyed with as many people as possible; and the principle of one course per person and one extra will ensure the right amount of dishes. The waiter can be asked for his personal recommendation. Prices for seasonal specialities and fresh seafood should be ascertained, for these items can be very expensive. Restaurants are very helpful in making suggestions for a balanced textured and tasty meal.

If you should be hosting a dinner with Chinese guests, the correct seating etiquette puts the guest of honour facing the door, with the host seated opposite. A local Hong Kong tradition, of never turning a fish over when eating it, is a superstition of the fishing community, who fear that a fishing boat will capsize at sea. Fruit and hot towels will indicate the end of the meal and Chinese guests do not expect to linger at table beyond this stage.

The ordinary man-in-the-street will take his meals at the street-side noodle stalls and snack shops. A popular, cheap local outdoor eating venue is the **Poor Man's Nightclub**, beyond the Macau Ferry Terminus, where dozens of makeshift stalls appear each evening to serve all sorts of seafood, rice dishes and noodle soups. Simply point out what you fancy and sit down. Both food and bill will eventually appear. A more refined, typically Cantonese style of eating is 'taking tea' (*yum char*) with *dim sum*. Restaurants serving these small snacks are warm and friendly, and are packed out from early morning till lunch

One of Aberdeen's many floating eateries: the Jumbo Fish Restaurant

time. The delicacies are wheeled around the restaurant in trollies. Simply indicate which delicacy you would like from the passing trolley lady, who will place the dish or steamed basket before you and mark the card on your table appropriately. Tea is served throughout.

Just a few of the popular *dim sum* dishes are listed below.

Cha Shiu Bau: steamed
barbecued pork bun
Shiu Mai: steamed minced
shrimp and pork dumplings
Har Gau: steamed shrimp
dumplings
Tsun Guen: spring rolls
Pai Gwat: steamed spareribs
with red pepper sauce
Ho Yip Fan: steamed fried rice
wrapped in lotus leaf
Jar Wan Tun: deep fried
dumplings with sweet and sour
sauce
Nor Mai Chi: coconut snowball

Hung Dow Sa: sweet red bean
soup
Daan Tart: egg custard tart

Cantonese
The foremost Chinese cuisine in
Hong Kong is Cantonese style,
originating in the nearby
province of Guangdong. Dishes
emphasise fresh ingredients and
natural flavour and colour.
Steaming and stir frying are
favoured and a minimum of oil is
used. They also have a tasty
barbecued meat tradition. The

FOOD AND DRINK

Baked mud-crab, one of Hong Kong's seafood-based Chinese dishes

province's long South China Sea coastline is rich in seafood and many restaurants keep tanks of live fish, crabs and shellfish. A popular sub-category of Cantonese food is *Chiu Chow* cuisine, originating in the Swatow (Shantou) region of north-eastern Guangdong province. The piquant flavourings of seafood, goose and duck are delicious. *Chiu Chow* meals begin and end with thimble-size cups of strong Iron Goddess tea. Local seafood specialities can also be enjoyed on the floating restaurants near Aberdeen, and at the villages of Lei Yue Mun and Lau Fau Shan in the New Territories.

Below is a selection of Cantonese restaurants:–
Chiuchow Garden Restaurant, Jardine House, Connaught Road Central (tel. 5258246) and Tsimshatsui Centre, 2nd Floor, Tsim Sha Tsui East, Kowloon (tel. 3688772). An extensive menu of *Chiu Chow* specialities which include fried satay beef, steamed pomfret fish with soya bean sauce, lemon duck soup, and roast goose with vinegar and garlic.
Jade Garden Restaurant, 1st Floor, Swire House, Des Voeux Road Central, Hong Kong (tel. 5239966); Star House, 4th Floor, Tsim Sha Tsui, Kowloon (tel. 7226888); and 1 Hysan Avenue, Causeway Bay, Hong Kong (tel. 5779332). Service is matter of fact and speedy with menus of

standard Cantonese dishes and seasonal delicacies, particularly seafood. These include barbecued pork, deep-fried stuffed crab claws, fillet of fish in lemon sauce, sautéed spiced prawns and the ever popular beggar's chicken baked in mud (this must be pre-ordered).

King Bun Restaurant, 158 Queen's Road Central, Hong Kong (tel. 5434256/5432223). Huge, noisy, and very popular with locals, this is considered one of the all-round best Cantonese restaurants in town. It serves excellent sweet and sour pork, barbecued duck, roast pork ribs, and minced pigeon. To appreciate the menu, go with a Cantonese friend.

Luk Yu Restaurant, 26 Stanley Street, Central, Hong Kong (tel. 5235464). Famed for its old teahouse atmosphere since 1925, it serves excellent *dim sum*. There are no English menus but the waiters are helpful and recommend seasonal specials.

Pak Lok Chiuchow Restaurant, 23–25 Hysan Avenue, Causeway Bay, Hong Kong (tel. 5774051). Concentrates on excellent food rather than refined service or surroundings. Heavily patronised and table bookings will not be held if you come late. Order fresh steamed crab (which will be shown to you live for your approval before cooking), roast goose and fried goose blood, crystal fried chicken, vegetables with Yunnan ham and unusual *E-fu* noodles served with vinegar and sugar.

Tai Woo Restaurant, 17–19 Wellington Street, Central, Hong Kong (tel. 5245618), 27 Percival

Street, Causeway Bay, Hong Kong (tel. 8939882); and 20–22a Granville Road, Tsim Sha Tsui, Kowloon (tel. 7398813). Excellent Cantonese dishes and *dim sum* make this group of restaurants popular for family banquets. Try braised cuttlefish, braised beef, crispy beancurd rolls and vegetarian hotpot.

Yung Kee Restaurant, 36–40 Wellington Street, Central, Hong Kong (tel. 5221624). A restaurant of long-standing high repute whose seafood—pomfret with chilli and black bean sauce, scallops, and grilled prawns—is recommended. Special winter dishes include snake soup with preserved duck.

Peking

This is a substantial cuisine, suited to the colder climes of China's northern capital, and influenced by the tastes of the court. Peking duck is the most famous delicacy and the golden roasted bird is shown to the table for approval before slicing. It is eaten wrapped up in thin pancakes with a sprig of spring onion and cucumber. Mongolian hot pot, served with a sauce mixed from seven ingredients and sesame rolls, is a winter favourite. Beggar's chicken is a speciality of many Peking restaurants in Hong Kong. Dumplings, noodles and steamed breads are preferred staples. If planning to eat Peking duck or beggar's chicken it is best to advise the restaurant when you book your table to avoid disappointment.

American Restaurant, 20 Lockhart Road, Wanchai, Hong Kong (tel. 5277277). An unlikely

FOOD AND DRINK

name for a restaurant with good
and reliable Peking dishes:
Peking duck, onion bread, chilli
prawns, shredded pork with
green pepper, diced chicken
with soya bean sauce, and
Tsientsin cabbage in chicken oil.
Prices are most reasonable but
book in advance.

Peking Garden, Alexandra
House, Des Voeux Road Central,
Hong Kong (tel. 5266456); Star
House, 3rd Floor, Tsim Sha Tsui,
Kowloon (tel. 3698211); and
Excelsior Hotel Shopping
Arcade, Causeway Bay, Hong
Kong (tel. 5266456). These
restaurants are reliable and
smart. Guests always enjoy the
chef's nightly demonstrations in
the skill of noodle making. Their
menus include cold meat,
famous Peking duck, duck soup,
smoked chicken, fried minced
pork with Chinese pickles, and
grilled mutton with spring onion.

Pine and Bamboo Restaurant, 30
Leighton Road, Causeway Bay
(tel. 5774914). This restaurant
serves authentic Mongolian hot
pot during the winter. The
Peking style is to order one kind
of meat only, either mutton or
beef, but the Cantonese
adaptation includes meat, fish
and chicken. The thin slivers of
meat are literally rinsed in broth
in the charcoal heated hot pot, to
which is added vegetables,
beancurd and noodles. After
cooking the meat is dipped into
a seven-flavour sauce and eaten
with sesame rolls. Typical
Peking dishes are also served.

Spring Deer Restaurant, 42 Mody
Road, 1st Floor, Kowloon (tel.
3664012/7233673). Locals prefer
this restaurant, considering its
Peking duck the best available.

Also try the chicken with chilli
and sweet peppers, noodles,
and sour-hot chilli prawns.

Shanghai
Shanghainese food tends to be
oily, rich and with a tendency
towards sweetness. Steamed
dumplings are traditional fare,
but seasonal specialities, such as
eels with garlic and freshwater
'hairy' crabs are delicious
autumn treats. These small crabs
are flown down live in huge
quantities from Shanghai—the
females, with their fat roe, are
more expensive than the males.
Hot ginger-flavoured tea is
served at the end of a crab feast.

Great Shanghai Restaurant, 26
Prat Avenue, 1st Floor, Kowloon
(tel. 3668158). A friendly and
comfortable restaurant, much
esteemed by gourmets of
Shanghainese cuisine. Its
drunken chicken (cold chicken
pieces flavoured with coriander
and yellow rice wine) is a
speciality of the house, as are its
eel dishes.

Shanghai Garden Restaurant,
Hutchison House, 10 Harcourt
Road, Central, Hong Kong (tel.
5238322) and 1st Floor,
Hennessy Centre, 500 Hennessy
Road, Causeway Bay, Hong
Kong (tel. 5779996). Yangtse
River dishes and seafood—
sautéed scallops with
vegetables, stewed shrimps with
tomato sauce and crispy rice,
steamed fish—as well as
steamed and fried dumplings,
served in elegant surroundings.

Sichuan
The hot, spicy cuisine of this
western province of China is one
of the four main styles of Chinese
cooking and is famous world-

wide, as its piquancy appeals to many palates. Peppers, coriander, ginger and garlic are basic ingredients.

Kam Chuen Lau, 4 Observatory Road, Tsim Sha Tsui, Kowloon (tel. 3675629). The Sichuan (or Szechuan)-style camphor wood and tea leaf smoked duck is this restaurant's speciality, along with other dishes such as fried shrimps with salt, deep fried beef with chilli and celery, and Sichuan bacon and leeks.

Sichuan Gardens, 3rd Floor, Gloucester Tower, The Landmark, Central, Hong Kong (tel. 5214433). Very good but expensive. Their menu offers crispy fried shredded beef with chilli, Yunnan ham and lotus-seeds in honey sauce, fried spiced spare-ribs, hot *mapo* beancurd and delicious camphor wood and tea smoked duck.

Sze Chuan Lau, 466 Lockhart Road, Causeway Bay, Hong Kong (tel. 8919027). In this well established restaurant, the service is brisk and efficient and prices reasonable. Hot red lychee tea is served to each guest as well as hot cabbage and sweet cucumber pickles as starters. Try the silver thread

Cuttlefish and octopuses among the delicacies on display in a restaurant larder

steamed bread rolls or fried
onion bread instead of rice—
also frog's leg dishes (seasonal),
braised beef in chilli and
mashed red bean pancake for
dessert.

Vegetarian
The Buddhist and Taoist
qualities of restraint and purity
lie at the heart of Chinese
vegetarian cooking. Beancurd is
widely used and often made to
look like meat. Chinese
vegetarian meals are light and
filling and aesthetically pleasing.
Buddhist monks are frequently to
be seen eating in these
restaurants.
Bodhi Vegetarian Restaurant, 388
Lockhart Road, Causeway Bay,
Hong Kong (tel. 5732155) and 56
Cameron Road, Tsim Sha Tsui,
Kowloon (tel. 7392222). Serves a
wide variety of Cantonese-style
vegetarian dishes.
Vegi Food Kitchen, 8 Cleveland
Street, Causeway Bay, Hong
Kong (tel. 8906660). A small
restaurant, always well
patronised, where the service is
both pleasant and helpful.
Delicious stuffed black
mushrooms, beancurd dishes
and beancurd skin rolls.
Wishful Cottage, 336 Lockhart
Road, Wanchai, Hong Kong (tel.
5735645). With Ming dynasty-
style lanterns and decorated
pillars, this restaurant looks like
a Buddhist temple. Vegetarian
dim sum dishes—dumplings
with spring onion, taro,
mushroom and bean sprout
stuffings—are popular at
lunchtime. Try also the dried
mushroom with walnut meat,
Lohan noodles and beancurd
dishes.

*Meats laid out at market, ready for
the Chinese New Year*

Asian
Hong Kong could be described
as a cross-roads of Asian cuisine
for there are restaurants serving
authentic national dishes from all
parts of the region. Even
Japanese food, usually
notoriously expensive, is
affordable here. Korean
barbecued beef, sharp and
spicy Thai and Vietnamese
soups and salads, and curries
from Indonesia, Burma, India and

Sri Lanka, make a pleasant change from Chinese food. Both the **Spice Market** in the Ocean Terminal, Kowloon (tel. 7306238) and **Spices** at 109 Repulse Bay Road, Hong Kong (tel. 81222711) have menus offering a cross-section of southeast Asian cuisine.

Indonesian
Java Rijstafel, 38 Hankow Road, Tsim Sha Tsui, Kowloon (tel. 3671230). A traditional Indonesian rice table buffet is served each luncheon, and this includes fish sambal, spiced beef, vegetables with coconut milk and chicken curry.

Shinta Indonesian Club, 1/F, 36–44 Queen's Road East, Wanchai, Hong Kong (tel. 5274974). There is not much attempt at atmosphere in this restaurant, but the satays, brought with little charcoal burners to your table, are very tasty, as is their *gado-gado* salad, *nasi goreng* rice, spiced Rendang beef and chilli fried prawns. Prices are most reasonable.

FOOD AND DRINK

Indian

Ashoka, 57 Wyndham Street, Central, Hong Kong (tel. 5249623). The selection of food from Kashmir and the Punjab at the Ashoka has made it a long-time favourite among lovers of Indian food. Apart from dishes such as tandoori chicken, beef and mutton curries and vegetable kofta and masala, the restaurant serves an assortment of meat or vegetarian dishes on a tray, which is perfect for a single diner.

New Delhi Restaurant, Mezz. Floor, 52 Cameron Road, Tsim Sha Tsui, Kowloon (tel. 3664611). Here you can order hot, medium or mild curries according to your taste. The tandoori house specialities are a mild spicy barbecued 'Chicken Old Delhi' and 'Chicken New Delhi', and a selection of stuffed paratha breads.

Japanese

Tomowa Japanese Restaurant, 6 Percival Street, Causeway Bay, Hong Kong (tel. 8336339). Diners may choose the ground floor area if they wish to eat at a counter, or the first floor if they want a comfortable booth. The Tomowa has excellent food in authentic surroundings. Try the *sushi* and *tappanyaki* dinners, cuttlefish with crab eggs, lobster, live prawns and seasonal vegetables.

Yagiu Restaurant, 13–17 Stanley Street, Central, Hong Kong (tel. 5239590). An unpretentious restaurant where the prices are most reasonable—for Japanese food, that is. One may sit at the *sushi* bar, around *tappanyaki* tables, or take a small cubicle.

The menu offers a range of set dinners as well as *à la carte* ordering and, of course, hot Japanese rice wine (*saki*).

Korean

Arirang Korean Restaurant, 76 Morrison Hill Road, Happy Valley, Hong Kong (tel. 5723027) and 9 Sutton Court, Ground Floor, Harbour City, 19 Canton Road, Kowloon (tel. 3692667). The traditional Korean barbecue, cooked at your table, always makes for a friendly and pleasant evening's dining, and these restaurants offer some 20 different types of marinated meat and seafood.

Koreana, 1 Paterson Street, Causeway Bay, Hong Kong (tel. 5775145). This has a pleasant, smoky atmosphere, and the hot pepper cabbage (*kimchee*), served with each meal, soon raises one's body temperature! Cook your own marinated chicken, beef, pork or shrimp barbecue at the table.

Thai

Golden Elephant Thai Restaurant, Unit 3, Barnton Court, Ground Floor, Harbour City, Phase 1, Tsim Sha Tsui, Kowloon (tel. 3692733). All the chefs are trained in Thailand and the atmosphere is authentic. Specialities include sliced boneless goose, spicy and sour abalone salad, oyster omelette and charcoal grilled chicken.

Golden Poppy, Henan Building, 90–93 Jaffe Road, Wanchai, Hong Kong (tel. 5283128). A spacious restaurant with a choice of over 100 true Thai dishes and a lunchtime buffet. The service is friendly and helpful. Excellent

Chinese biscuits. Sweet and savoury snacks are set out on street stalls

sour and spicy prawn soup, chilli or curry crab, steamed fish, and green papaya salad.
Supatna's, 50 D'Aguilar Street, Lan Kwai Fong, Central, Hong Kong (tel. 5225073). A popular new Thai restaurant with character. The appetising menu includes fish cakes, spicy and sour prawn soup, green curry with roasted duck, spicy squid salad and Thai fried rice.

Vietnamese
Paterson Vietnamese Restaurant, 10 Cleveland Street, Causeway Bay, Hong Kong (tel. 8906146). The waitresses are usually a little overworked so the service can be slow, but the food is good. Try beef cooked in seven different ways, fried salt and pepper crab, Vietnamese spring rolls (which are served with lettuce leaves and fresh mint) or hot and sour fish head soup.
Vietnam City Vietnamese Restaurant, 3rd Floor, Elizabeth House, 250 Gloucester Road, Causeway Bay, Hong Kong (tel. 8336882) and Lower Ground Floor, Energy Plaza, 92 Granville Road, Kowloon (tel. 3667880). The Elizabeth House branch has created a garden atmosphere

FOOD AND DRINK

and the chef's recommendations
include roasted suckling pig,
jumbo prawn salad, seafood
curry and crispy chicken. The
Kowloon branch includes a
number of seafood specialities
on its menu.

Western
Au Trou Normand, 6 Carnarvon
Road, Tsim Sha Tsui, Kowloon
(tel. 3668754). The French
owner/chef Bernard Vigneau
has been running this restaurant
for over 20 years and has
created a solid reputation. The
décor is rustic and the service
professional.
Bentley's Seafood Restaurant, B4
Basement, Prince's Building, Des
Voeux Road Central, Hong Kong
(tel. 8680881). A member of the
Bentley's Seafood Restaurant
chain of London, it recreates a
conservative and quiet British
atmosphere, which is reflected
in the menu—first class but
simple seafood dishes.
Café de Paris, 30–32 D'Aguilar
Street, Central, Hong Kong (tel.
5247421). Temperamental Chef
Maurice calls his restaurant 'a
corner of Paris in the heart of
Hong Kong', and this is no
exaggeration. Its chic décor,
high standard of cuisine and
good selection of wines make
this excellent value.
Chesa, Peninsula Hotel,
Salisbury Road, Tsim Sha Tsui,
Kowloon (tel. 3666251). Along
with **Gaddi's**, this is a leading
restaurant; the former serves
superb Swiss food and the latter
first class European dishes. Plush
and elegant surroundings, and,
of course, expensive. Gaddi's
special executive lunch menu is,
however, good value.

Jimmy's Kitchen, 1 Wyndham
Street, Central, Hong Kong (tel.
5265293); 100 Peak Road, The
Peak, Hong Kong (tel.
8497788); and 1st Floor, 29–39

*Taking refreshments in lofty
company in front of the Repulse Bay
Temple*

Ashley Road, Tsim Sha Tsui, Kowloon (tel. 3684027). Jimmy's Kitchen started as a seaman's café in Shanghai in the 1940s and moved to Hong Kong with its staff. The atmosphere in these restaurants is cosy and reassuring, and the menu contains a special blend of east

and west, reflecting its China-coast tradition. Prices are reasonable.

La Taverna, 34–38 Ashley Road, Tsim Sha Tsui, Kowloon (tel. 3691945) and 1st Floor, 24–30 Ice House Street, Central, Hong Kong (tel. 5228904). The atmosphere is typically Mediterranean and the Italian dishes, though erratic in quality, are fresh and appetising. Specialities are pizzas, seafood and desserts.

Pierrot, and **Grill Room**, Mandarin Oriental Hotel, Connaught Road, Central, Hong Kong (tel. 5220111). Very elegant and expensive, excellent and delicate service with dishes and wine to match.

Stanley's, 86–88 Stanley Main Street, Stanley, Hong Kong (tel. 8138873). Delightfully situated, overlooking Stanley Bay, this restaurant's Provençal-style French menu, though not extensive, is first class.

Drink

Drinking wine while composing poetry was the favoured pastime of the Chinese literati for centuries. Today drinking is still an important part of the enjoyment of a Chinese banquet. The standard Cantonese toast is *Yum sing!* (meaning 'Cheers!'). Traditionally golden yellow rice wine from Shaoxing is preferred. This sherry-like wine is aged in earthenware jars for up to seven years and is served warm from wine jugs and poured into small wine cups.

The fiery white *sorghum* liquor called *mao tai* is popular too, but in recent years, this special hard liquor from Kweichow province,

FOOD AND DRINK

Tea is always taken with Chinese meals. This herbal tea shop is in Hong Kong Island's Western District

and a favourite of the late Chairman Mao Tsetung, has become scarce and too expensive. So local people drink substitutes such as *fen jiu* (*fen chiew*) and *wu liang ye*. Unlike Shaoxing wine, these distilled liquors do not usually appeal to the western palate. Other Chinese wines, often sweet and unusual in flavour, include Green Bamboo Leaf Wine, Rose Nectar and Tiger Bone Papaya wine.

However, the most favoured drink with Chinese meals among the affluent Hong Kong people these days is French Cognac, and the territory is among the highest consumers of VSOP brandy in the world. European restaurants serve imported French, German, Italian and Australian wines. Cocktail bars and nightclubs serve an assortment of both traditional and creative cocktails. The local beer, San Miguel, is a lager-like brew, and is light and popular, but many imported beers are available.

SHOPPING

Three million tourists a year
cannot be wrong—Hong Kong is
an amazing place to shop. The
streets and alleys are jammed
with air-conditioned shops and
market stalls stocking an
overwhelming array of goods,
both imported and locally made.
Many goods are cheaper here
than in their place of origin, due
to duty free imports, and this
applies particularly to goods
from mainland China.

For those who love the challenge
of bargaining over prices, Hong
Kong is a delight which may
reward your time and
determination with more than
satisfactory value-for-money
purchases. But those who are
disinclined to haggle with
aggressive sales staff may find
the process irritating and
distasteful, and simply pay
roughly what is asked in the
interest of time-saving.

Once you are in Hong Kong it is
doubly important to shop around
on prices, for the same object
can vary widely in price. The
lowest price may not necessarily
mean the best quality—slightly
defective goods may be foisted
on you to make up for any big
discount.

Of the thousands of shops only
some 1,300 are members of the
Hong Kong Tourist Association
and display their red junk logo.
These stores are considered to
be highly reputable, but this
does not mean that Hong Kong
business people are not mostly
honest and conscientious. Your
purchases may be discussed
over proffered cigarettes or
cups of Chinese tea which lends

amiability to the negotiations!
Always check carefully that the
goods are packed before your
eyes and that you have received
exactly the component parts and
accessories you wanted. *Never*
pay a deposit on goods which
have to be fetched from the
warehouse; and check your
receipt carefully—once you
have accepted it you have very
little recourse. Ask for world-
wide guarantees where
possible.

*The Official Guide to Shopping,
Eating Out and Services*
published by the Hong Kong
Tourist Association is a
comprehensive introduction to
Hong Kong's shopping world.
There are three principal
shopping areas: downtown
Kowloon in Tsim Sha Tsui and
Tsim Sha Tsui East, Hong Kong
Island's Central District and the
Causeway Bay area. Having said
this, the Yau Ma Tei and Mong
Kok districts (accessible by
MTR) offer good bargains too.
Obviously, the more central the
shop, the more its massive rental
overheads affect prices. Trading
hours are usually from 10.00–
18.00 but many shops will stay
open till 19.30 or even 21.30 in
the evening.

Cameras and Optical Equipment

The latest models and
accessories are on sale in the
many, many shops dealing in this
trade. The staff are very
knowledgeable and anxious to
assist. Discounts of 10 per cent or
so can be arranged. To avoid
later disappointment, note that
the serial number of the
equipment checks out with the

SHOPPING

guarantee. Binoculars are
particularly good buys. James
Morgan has written a booklet
aptly named: *How to Avoid
Getting Ripped-Off in Hong
Kong Buying Cameras and Photo
Accessories*, which is available
at many bookstores.
Inexpensive and accurate eye
tests are carried out in the
optician stores and prescription
glasses and contact lenses can
be made in a very short time.
The cost is more than reasonable.

Electronic Equipment

There are sound systems galore
to tempt you, as well as all the
latest electronic games and
gadgetry of our age. Always
check the voltage of equipment
and the compatibility of VHS
systems. The trade in cheap
'fake' personal computers has
ended, and centres now stock
the widest choice of high quality
software.

Jewellery

Second in number only to
camera shops are jewellery
stores. Favourite targets of
smash-and-grab robbers, they
nonetheless do a flourishing
business. Local jewellery excels
in craftsmanship and design and
pieces can be custom made.
Prices are very competitive.
Gold and jade are traditionally
popular with Chinese buyers.
Translucent green or 'mutton fat'
white are particularly favoured
colours but jade also comes in
many other beautiful colours.
There are two types of jade:
jadeite—used in jewellery—
and nephrite for carvings. Most
of the high quality jade comes
from Burma. Kowloon's Jade
Market is an intriguing place to

*Hong Kong has shops crammed with
curios and reproduced 'antiques'*

buy cheap pieces of jade
jewellery.
The diamond trade in Hong
Kong is one of the world's
largest, so prices are low. For
detailed information on cut,
colour and carat weight contact
the **Diamond Importers
Association Ltd**, Room 1707,
17th Floor, Lane Crawford
House, 70 Queen's Road Central
(tel. 5235497).
A wide selection of pearls—
cultured, fresh-water and
baroque—ranges in price
according to quality and size.

Your choice of colouring—milk white, ivory, pale pink or grey—depends upon your preference. Pearls can be strung for you within hours. Semi-precious stones too are in abundance. The various branches of China Arts and Crafts sell attractive but conservative jewellery.

Clothing and Fabrics

The rag trade is still a mainstay of the Hong Kong economic miracle and the entire spectrum of ready-to-wear apparel, from the cheapest T-shirt to the most expensive high fashion European labels, is available, the latter being very popular with Japanese tourists. In recent years Hong Kong's own designers have earned international acclaim. Couturier boutiques are to be found, cheek by jowl, in the smart shopping complexes of the Landmark, Prince's Building and Swire House in Central, Hong Kong. In Kowloon the shopping arcades of the Peninsula and Regent Hotels are centres for international elegance. Two local designers have carved a world reputation: **Diane Freis** for lovely soft, uncrushable and colourful dresses and separates; and **Jenny Lewis**, who has an eye for old Chinese fabrics and embroideries, and creates beautiful gowns and jackets with strong oriental motifs.

Clothing with designer labels—jeans, men's shirts and sportswear—can be bought very cheaply in the street bazaars, particularly at Stanley Market, on the south side of Hong Kong Island.

Factory outlets sell their export overruns of knitwear, silk garments, leatherwear and accessories, from their factory premises in the dreary industrial districts of Kwun Tong, Lai Chi Kok or San Po Kong (accessible by MTR). Other factories have premises in downtown Kowloon and in Central, Hong Kong, and goods sell at wholesale prices. *The Complete Guide to Hong Kong Factory Bargains* by Diana Goetz, is updated every year and is on sale at bookshops. The HKTA also prints a useful listing.

Custom-tailored garments, for men and women, can be fitted and completed within a few days, though the workmanship may be better if the tailor can take a bit longer over them. Two or three fittings are advised. Garments can also be given to the tailor to copy. Usually a 10 per cent deposit will be asked once your measurements have been noted.

Tailoring shops have selections of fabrics for you to choose from. For a vast choice of British wools, cashmere, silks, cottons and synthetics, the narrow little lane known as 'Cloth Alley' or Wing On Street in Central is the place. Pure silks from China are available by the metre at the **Chinese Arts and Crafts** department stores, as well as

cotton and silk garments, embroideries and cashmere sweaters.

Shoes

Visitors can have shoes custom-made at reasonable prices. Fittings are desirable to ensure comfort and satisfaction. Ready-made local fashion shoes can be tried on at the numerous shoe-shops which trade side by side on a section of Wong Nai Chung Road, Happy Valley. Matching handbags make nice accessories.

Watches

Hong Kong's own watch industry produces attractive and accurate timepieces while the colony is a major importer of famous Swiss and Japanese brands. If choosing an expensive watch make sure that the serial number of the watch corresponds with its international guarantee, and try to make sure that the band is the original one.

Furniture

Hand carved teak, rosewood and blackwood furniture is made with a high degree of skill and taste and Chinese craftsmen can be seen at work in furniture shops on Queen's Road East and Hollywood Road on Hong Kong Island. Handsome dining suites, occasional tables, cupboards or camphor wood chests can be custom-made and safe shipment arranged.

In recent years the simple lines of Ming dynasty northern Chinese furniture have become more popular than the heavily carved pieces typical of southern China. Cane and rattan furniture is also made.

Carpets

Fine Chinese wool or silk carpets are often cheaper to buy here than in China. Hong Kong's own **Tai Ping Carpet Factory**, Lot No. 1687, Tai Ping Industrial Park, Ting Kok Road, Tai Po Market, New Territories (tel. 6565161 for an appointment) make quality carpets in modern or traditional designs and are happy to make to personal requirements. Other carpet shops specialise in antique tribal rugs from Persia and Afghanistan, or modern carpets from Pakistan and India.

Antiques

Hollywood Road and Wyndham Street in Central, Hong Kong, is the home of Asian antiques and art works. Galleries elegantly display antique paintings, furniture, imperial costumes, ivory, pottery and porcelain. Unfortunately, there are not many bargains these days, even

The temptation of the market stalls, with their fresh produce, can sometimes prove too much . . .

92

SHOPPING

Shops spill out onto the street in Hollywood Road and Bird Street

in the famous old 'Cat Street' (Upper Lascar Road) antique market. Antiques and modern reproductions frequently stand side by side.

Treasures continue to be smuggled from the mainland and it is sometimes possible to find painted pottery pots which are over 2,000 years old.

On Kowloon side, Charlotte Horstmann in the Ocean Terminal has a reputation for genuine, quality antiques.

Handicrafts

Delicate paper cuts, peasant woodcuts, weavings, embroideries, puppets, lacquer, stone carvings, linen tableware and basketry are just some of the traditional handicrafts from China to be found at the **Chinese Arts and Crafts** department stores, and at **Mountain Folk Craft** shops on both sides of the harbour.

The Banyan Tree and **Amazing Grace** deal in furnishings and hand crafted decorative objects which come from various countries in Asia.

ACCOMMODATION

Most of the territory's hotels are first class, both in décor, service and facilities. The lobbies are elegantly and lavishly decorated. Many are well appointed, offering stunning views of Hong Kong harbour. Hotels maintain a 90 per cent occupancy rate all year round. Rooms are air-conditioned with bathroom, TV, mini-bar and refrigerator.

Hotel restaurants serve Chinese and Western cuisine of a high standard. Some of the colony's very best restaurants are located in the top hotels. Conference rooms, business centres, swimming pools, private dining halls and discos are among the many facilities Hong Kong hotels offer.

The more moderately priced hotels also tend to have good service and pleasant, small rooms, but the likelihood is that they will have no view.

Room rates quoted below are subject to a 15 per cent tax and these prices are obviously subject to change.

Hong Kong Island

Excelsior Hotel, 281 Gloucester Road, Causeway Bay (tel. 5767365). A very comfortable hotel, with high standards of service, conveniently situated in a busy shopping and restaurant area. Its sports facilities include tennis courts and a health club. It has three restaurants and three bars, of which the Dickens Bar is a popular spot for residents. The hotel runs a mini-bus service to Central District. It has 926 rooms which range from HK$1,050–HK$1,500 a double.

Furama Inter-Continental, 1 Connaught Road, Central (tel. 5255111). One of Central's leading hotels, close to the Star Ferry. Its revolving restaurant on the top floor is a special attraction and the hotel's ballroom is heavily booked for exhibitions and conferences. There are four restaurants and three bars. Most of its 571 rooms have a view and rates are HK$1,300–HK$1,450 a double.

Harbour Hotel, 116–122 Gloucester Road, Wanchai (tel. 5748211). A moderately priced hotel on the waterfront in the nightclub area of Wanchai with a relaxed atmosphere. Its Chinese restaurant serves good, plain dishes. Other facilities include a bar and nightclub. The hotel's 200 rooms are priced at HK$680–HK$850 a double.

Hilton Hotel, 2 Queen's Road, Central (tel. 5233111). Situated in the heart of Central District, the Hilton has four restaurants, including a very popular grill room, elegant top-storey Chinese restaurant and pleasant dining around a spacious pool. It has a business centre and a health club. The Hilton runs harbour cruises aboard its own beautiful brigantine, the *Wah Fu*. It has 800 rooms at HK$1,540–HK$1,700 a double.

Lee Gardens Hotel, Hysan Avenue, Causeway Bay (tel. 8953311). An 809-room hotel in Causeway Bay, close to shops and nightlife. Several restaurants, bar and coffee shop give efficient and pleasant service. Room prices at HK$950–HK$1,200 a double.

Mandarin Oriental Hotel, 5 Connaught Road, Central (tel.

ACCOMMODATION

5220111). Part of a hotel group which operates some of the best hotels in Asia, the Mandarin is considered the leading one on the island. Apart from a health club, swimming pool and business centre, its Clipper Lounge is popular for afternoon tea, and the clientele of the Captain's Bar is made up of the community's leading businessmen. Restaurants include an excellent French Restaurant, and a grill room. Its 565 rooms are priced at HK$1,500–HK$1,900 a double.

New Harbour Hotel, 41–49 Hennessy Road, Wanchai (tel. 8611166). The 173 rooms are small and functional, as is the restaurant, bar and coffee shop. Situated in the centre of Wanchai, the hotel's room rates cover a price range of HK$580–HK$850 a double.

Park Lane Radisson Hotel, 310 Gloucester Road, Causeway Bay (tel. 8903355). A spacious hotel close to Food Street and Causeway Bay shopping, its various facilities include several restaurants, coffee shop, disco, and sauna. It has 850 rooms. Prices: HK$950–HK$1,400 a double.

Victoria Hotel, Shun Tak Centre, 200 Connaught Road, Central (tel. 5407228). This very pleasant Central hotel can boast unobstructed views of the harbour as well as a number of facilities such as restaurants, health club, business centre, swimming pool, and music room. Accommodation in the hotel consists of 330 small apartments and 540 rooms. Prices: HK$1,300–HK$1,600 a double.

The distinctive twin towers of the Victoria Hotel and Shun Tak Centre in Central District

Kowloon

Ambassador Hotel, 26 Nathan Road, Tsim Sha Tsui (tel. 3666321). Well placed in downtown Kowloon, the hotel is popular with tour-groups. Service staff are familiar and friendly. Facilities include a nightclub bar, coffee shop and two restaurants. Its 315 rooms are priced HK$1,080–HK$1,380 a double.

Tsui (tel. 3693111). A hotel with a high reputation for management, with a business centre, pool, sauna, three restaurants and bars. It has 599 rooms priced at HK$900–HK$1,480 a double.

Holiday Inn Harbour View, 70 Mody Road, Tsim Sha Tsui East (tel. 7215161). Facilities at this harbour view hotel include a business centre, bars, pool and health club. The food served in its five restaurants is first class. The hotel has 600 rooms priced between HK$1,150–HK$1,900 a double.

The Hong Kong (Omni) Hotel, 3 Canton Road, Tsim Sha Tsui (tel. 7360088). This is a very popular hotel, with low-key elegance, and perfectly situated for the Star Ferry and Ocean Terminal shopping complex. The hotel has a pool, health club and three restaurants serving excellent food. Its 790 rooms are priced at HK$950–HK$1,900 a double.

Hyatt Regency Hotel, 67 Nathan Road, Tsim Sha Tsui (tel. 3111234). A first class hotel in the heart of Kowloon, with business centre, nightclub, bars and four restaurants; among them Hugo's, which is considered excellent. Rates for its 723 rooms range from HK$1,380–HK$1,630 a double.

Kowloon Hotel, 19–21 Nathan Road, Tsim Sha Tsui (tel. 3698698). A subsidiary of the Peninsula Group of Hotels, but the rooms are not as large as its grand parent hotel. Facilities include two restaurants, coffee shop, bar and business centre. It has 707 rooms priced between HK$770–HK$820 a double.

Marco Polo (Omni) Hotel,

Empress Hotel, 17–19 Chatham Road, Tsim Sha Tsui (tel. 3660211). An unpretentious hotel, conveniently situated. Rates for its 189 rooms range from HK$800–HK$950 a double.

Grand Hotel, 14 Carnarvon Road, Tsim Sha Tsui (tel. 3669331). A long established hotel in the centre of Kowloon; no frills, but reliable. It has two restaurants and a bar and its 194 rooms range in price from HK$720–HK$920 a double.

Holiday Inn Golden Mile Hotel, 46–52 Nathan Road, Tsim Sha

ACCOMMODATION

Convenient for high-flyers: the Regal Meridien Airport hotel

Canton Road, Tsim Sha Tsui (tel. 7360888). Like the Kowloon Hotel, a member of the Peninsula Group of Hotels, this waterfront hotel has a sports centre, health centre, pool, restaurants and bar. It has 441 rooms in the price range HK$1,100–HK$1,250 a double.

Miramar Hotel, 130 Nathan Road, Tsim Sha Tsui (tel. 3681111). A large hotel with three wings, which has been long established. In all it has some 11 restaurants, five bars, a supper club, and convention and business centres. Its 542 rooms range in price between HK$1,060–HK$1,160 a double.
Park Hotel, 61–65 Chatham Road, Tsim Sha Tsui (tel.

3661371). Well situated for shopping and popular with tour-groups. It has 450 large rooms within the price range HK$900–HK$1,100 a double.

Peninsula Hotel, Salisbury Road, Tsim Sha Tsui (tel. 3666251). Hong Kong's grand old hotel, famous for its style and service. Its five restaurants serve superb food and the lobby is a meeting place for the rich and famous. The hotel has 210 rooms in the price range HK$2,000–HK$2,300 a double.

Prince (Omni) Hotel, Canton Road, Tsim Sha Tsui (tel. 7361888). A harbour-fronting hotel, conveniently located, with pleasant rooms and business centre. It has 402 rooms ranging between HK$1,100–HK$1,250 a double.

Regal Meridien, 71 Mody Road, Tsim Sha Tsui East (tel. 7221818). Part of the Air France-Meridien chain of hotels, the hotel has several bars, a disco and five restaurants, one of which has excellent French cuisine. Its 590 rooms are priced HK$1,200–HK$1,680.

Regal Meridien Airport Hotel, Sa Po Road, Kowloon (tel. 7180333). This is the main airport hotel and is connected to the airport by a walkway. French cuisine; 384 rooms in the price range HK$1,000–HK$1,100 a double.

Regent Hotel, Salisbury Road, Tsim Sha Tsui (tel. 7211211). A deluxe hotel overlooking the harbour with a grand and spacious lobby. A health club, business centre and pool are among its facilities. It has five restaurants serving superb food. Price range for its 602 rooms HK$1,400–HK$2,200 a double.

Royal Garden Hotel, 69 Mody Road, Tsim Sha Tsui East (tel. 7215215). The central architectural theme of this hotel is a garden atrium, onto which rooms face. With 433 rooms, rates range from HK$1,050–HK$1,650 a double.

Shangri-La Hotel, 64 Mody Road, Tsim Sha Tsui East (tel. 7212111). A deluxe hotel with sumptuous decorations and all facilities—business centre, sauna, pool—and an elegant lobby with harbour view for drinks or afternoon tea. It has 719 rooms in the price range HK$1,650–HK$2,450 a double.

Sheraton Hotel, 20 Nathan Road, Tsim Sha Tsui (tel. 3691111). Centrally located, opposite the Peninsula Hotel, the disco and night club are very lively; and the hotel offers a business centre and pool as well (922 rooms). Prices: HK$1,300–HK$1,800.

New Territories

Regal Riverside Plaza, Tai Chung Kiu Road, Sha Tin (tel. 6497878). Facilities in this new hotel include pool, health centre and disco. A hotel bus shuttle service operates to Sha Tin railway station and downtown Tsim Sha Tsui. Rates for the 830 rooms are between HK$800–HK$1,000 a double.

Hostels and Guesthouses

Caritas Lodge, 134 Boundary Street, Kowloon (tel. 3365211)

Chungking House, 4th Floor, Block A, Chungking Mansions, 40 Nathan Road, Kowloon (tel. 3665362)

YMCA, Harbour View International House, 4 Harbour Road, Wanchai, Hong Kong (tel. 5201111)

NIGHTLIFE AND ENTERTAINMENT

The Performing Arts

Hong Kong today has quite a rich cultural life and very modern facilities in which to present local and international performances. Western and Chinese classical music concerts are performed by professional Hong Kong orchestras – the Philharmonic and the Chinese Orchestra—and by visiting world-famous orchestras and soloists.

Traditional Chinese operas are staged before enthusiastic audiences, and visiting troupes from China perform in regional styles. Visitors will enjoy the magnificent costume colours, the make-up, and the highly stylised movements which substitute stage props, but may find the singing styles foreign to the ear. Peking opera is often full of amazing acrobatic and martial feats, but Cantonese opera can be slow moving. If you attend a performance, don't be embarrassed about leaving after an hour if you feel that you have had enough. Chinese puppet shows are also held.

The month-long Hong Kong Arts Festival, held each year in January to February, is a cultural highlight of dance, theatre, mime and music.

Pop concerts are huge events staged at the Coliseum in Kowloon, attended by thousands of fans, be the performers local Cantonese, Taiwanese or Western pop stars.

Tickets for performances are available at URBTIX (tel. 5739595) and TICKET-MATE

Dancing and acrobatics are part of the spectacular shows often held during festivals in Hong Kong

(tel. 8339300) outlets, or at the box offices of the City Hall (tel. 5739595), Arts Centre (tel. 8230200) or Centre of Performing Arts (tel. 8231500), depending on the sponsors. Cinemas screen Western and Chinese films, but Hong Kong-made Chinese *kung fu* movies are the most popular. Films are all sub-titled. Screening times are published daily in the English language newspapers.

Art exhibitions are normally held in private galleries, the Arts Centre and the City Hall. To obtain information of what's on in Hong Kong check the daily newspapers, the weekly publication *Orient*, or the monthly *City News* (available at the City Hall free of charge).

The English Media

There are two English and two Chinese language commercial TV stations and five English language radio programmes. The two main local daily newspapers in English are the *South China Morning Post* and *Hong Kong Standard*. Asian editions of the *Wall Street Journal* and *International Herald Tribune* are printed in Hong Kong.

Nightlife

Hong Kong's nightlife is not as obviously flamboyant as that of Bangkok or Manila but it is very lively: English style pubs, elegant bars, strobe-lit discos, hostess clubs, girlie bars, and massage parlours. Wanchai is famous for its girlie bars—but be warned, this form of

NIGHTLIFE AND ENTERTAINMENT

companionship is often very expensive.

At the **Public Square Street Night Market** in Yau Ma Tei (a short walk from the Jordan Road MTR station) visitors may wander about amid fortune tellers, food stalls, story tellers, and miscellaneous vendors. A similar evening market, the **Poor Man's Nightclub**, is situated near the Macau Ferry Pier on Hong Kong Island.

Check your hotel for evening dinner-dance boat cruises which are operated by several tour companies. The HKTA runs nightly **Yum Sing—Night on The Town** tours.

Up-market Pubs and Bars

Hong Kong
Brown's Wine Bar, 104–206, Tower 2, Exchange Square, Central.
Bull and Bear, Hutchison House, Chater Rd, Central.
Captain's Bar, Mandarin Hotel, Central.
Clipper Lounge, Mandarin Hotel, Central.
Dickens Bar, Excelsior Hotel, Causeway Bay.
Dragon Boat Bar, Hilton Hotel, Central.
Joe Bananas, Shiu Nam Building, 23 Luard Rd, Wanchai.
The Jockey, 108A Shopping Arcade, Swire House, Connaught Rd, Central.

Kowloon
Bar City, B–2, New World Centre, Salisbury Rd, Tsim Sha Tsui.
The Blacksmith's Arms, 16 Minden Ave, Tsim Sha Tsui.
Chin Chin Bar, Hyatt Regency Hotel, 67 Nathan Rd, Tsim Sha Tsui.

Grammy's Lounge, 2A Hart Ave, Tsim Sha Tsui.
Gun Bar, The Hong Kong Hotel, 3 Canton Rd, Tsim Sha Tsui.
Harry's Bar Hong Kong, 6–8A Prat Ave, Tsim Sha Tsui.
Sky Lounge, Penthouse, Sheraton Hotel, 20 Nathan Rd, Tsim Sha Tsui.
White Stag, 72 Canton Rd, Tsim Sha Tsui.

Discos

Hong Kong
Disco Disco, 38 D'Aguilar St, Central.
Nineteen 97, 9 Lan Kwai Fong, Central.
Talk of the Town, 34/F, The Excelsior Hotel, Causeway Bay.

Kowloon
Canton, 161–163 World Finance Centre, North Tower, Harbour City, Tsim Sha Tsui.
Faces, New World Hotel, Salisbury Rd, Tsim Sha Tsui.
Falcon, Royal Garden Hotel, Tsim Sha Tsui East.

Hostess Clubs & Bars

Hong Kong
Dai-Ichi Club, 1/F, Harbour View Mansion, 257 Gloucester Rd, Causeway Bay.
Club Celebrity, 175–191 Lockhart Rd, Wanchai.
New Tonnochy Nightclub, 1–5 Tonnochy Rd, Wanchai.

Kowloon
Bottoms Up, B/F, 14–16 Hankow Rd, Tsim Sha Tsui.
Club Deluxe, L–301, New World Centre Office Building, Salisbury Rd, Tsim Sha Tsui.
Club Volvo, Lower G/F, Mandarin Plaza, 14 Science Museum Rd, Tsim Sha Tsui East.

WEATHER AND WHEN TO GO

The best time to visit Hong Kong is during the months of October to December. The clear blue skies, pleasant day temperatures—mid-20s C (mid-70s F) and evening lows of 15–10 degrees C (60–50 degrees F)—low humidity and rainfall make Hong Kong's autumn weather ideal for tourist activities.
Winter is short and mild. January and February may bring cold fronts which can reduce the temperature to around 10 degrees C (50 degrees F) while temperatures are known to drop to freezing in parts of the New Territories.
Rising temperatures in March and April bring heavy mists, low clouds and clammy damp. Residents turn on their wardrobe heaters to prevent

The other side of Hong Kong: the forests, mountains, parklands and rice fields of the New Territories

WEATHER AND WHEN TO GO

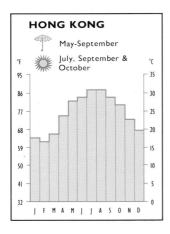

HONG KONG

May–September

July, September & October

mildew as their apartment walls stream with condensation. The thick mists can bring delays at airports and ferry terminals. The hot long summer takes hold in May and continues through till August. During these months temperatures average 30–32 degrees C (85–88 degrees F), with little respite at night. Humidity is high (90 per cent) and the sun strong. The monsoon season brings heavy rains, and 80 per cent of Hong Kong's rainfall occurs during these summer months, particularly in June and July.

Typhoons and severe tropical storms can plague the territory from July onwards. Though it is rare to receive a direct hit, torrential downpours cause landslides and flooding and gale force winds may bring down trees and scaffolding. With their approach the Royal Observatory issues regular progress bulletins on radio and TV, and typhoon signals are hoisted throughout

the territory. For up-to-date information telephone the Tropical Cyclone Warning Signal Enquiries Offices (tel. 3690066). The hoisting of the No 3 signal requires residents to put up storm shutters and for fishing boats to make for safe harbour in typhoon shelters. The No 8 signal demands that all schools, businesses and offices close their doors to allow the public time to get home before public transport is brought to a halt. No 10, luckily rarely raised, indicates a direct hit with wind strengths of 64 knots or higher.

Clothing

Lightweight clothes are a must for summer sightseeing but a jacket or cardigan is advisable for dining out, as hotels and restaurants are air-conditioned and can be chilly. An umbrella is more useful than a raincoat during the hot months due to the high humidity.

Men may be required to wear a jacket and tie in some of the city's smart bars and restaurants. Warmer clothing—jackets, sweaters and a light overcoat—are necessary during the cooler months between December and March.

Local ladies delight in taking the opportunity of cooler weather to bring their fur coats out of cold storage, but this is a status symbol rather than a climatic necessity.

Suits are worn by Hong Kong's male business community, and the fashion-conscious young women are well dressed. However, the tourist will find casual dress both comfortable and acceptable.

HOW TO BE A LOCAL

Unlike other Asian countries, like Japan or Thailand, where traditional ways of behaviour are still the norm, in the social round Hong Kong Chinese have a Westernised sophistication. International standards of behaviour are adhered to, so that a tourist will break the ice by shaking hands, and engaging in polite exchanges about family, health, occupation and interests, just as one would elsewhere. Underneath, a traditional complicated Confucian ethic of social inter-relationships – which has dominated all Chinese societies since the 5th century BC – still exists among the Chinese themselves. However, foreigners are not expected to involve themselves in these subtleties unless they have married into Chinese families. For it is a lifetime study in itself. Hong Kong's cosmopolitanism enables the visitor to feel enveloped in an exciting and vibrant Chinese society without the distress of feeling that you are giving inadvertent offence.

A fortune teller maps out the future during the Bun Festival

SPECIAL EVENTS

Chinese Religion and Festivals

Though some Chinese are pure Buddhists, the majority practise a mixture of Taoism and Buddhism, worshipping a range of deities whose intercessionary powers are sought on the problems of daily life. The Confucian ethic of ancestor worship is very important, and most households have a family altar at which incense is burnt and offerings made regularly.

In spite of the apparent modernism of Hong Kong society, it is still a very traditional one, and Chinese festivals are a

An elaborate traditional costume, with its carefully embroidered motifs and ornate head-dress

colourful and important adjunct to life, especially to New Territories villagers and boat people. Temple offerings of food (wine, roast chickens, roast suckling pig, dyed eggs, fruits) and incense are obligatory at festivals, which are always boisterous and happy occasions. Well-loved operas are performed in giant mat sheds erected for the occasion. Lion and dragon dances often form part of the celebrations. Dates of festivals are based on the lunar calendar.

The major festivals are mentioned below, but there are numerous smaller ones which are equally interesting, and it is worth enquiring whether there is a festival going on during your stay. Exact dates can vary widely, and a general guide only can be given.

January/February

Chinese New Year (late January or early February). The most important of all annual festivals, as it is a time for family reunion, ancestor worship, present giving and feasting. The Kitchen God is sent off to report on the year's happenings (but his mouth is first smeared with sticky sweets so that he will only be flattering). All debts are paid, and red good luck couplets are placed by the doorway. New clothes are donned and visits made to friends and family. At special flower markets crowds rush to buy peach flower blossoms (representing longevity), orange trees (prosperity) and other 'lucky' flowers. Tens of thousands of Hong Kong residents return to their home villages in China for this celebration. A huge

A Chinese juggler finds an excuse to put her feet up during a festival performance

fireworks display is held in the harbour and the city is bedecked in coloured lights, as it is for Christmas. Shops are normally closed for three days. The celebrations officially come to and end on the 15th day of the first lunar month with the hanging of paper lanterns at the Lantern Festival.

April

Ching Ming. People in Hong Kong and Macau remember their ancestors on this day in early April, visiting family graves to clean them up and making offerings of food, flowers and incense before them. It is an occasion which dates back to the 3rd century BC.

April/May

Cheung Chau Bun Festival. Dates for this festival are chosen by divination, and celebrations go on for six days, culminating in a wonderful procession in which children are wired into astounding postures. Extraordinary 60-ft (18m) high Bun towers dominate the temple square and nearby matsheds house exquisite giant paper gods. The island's inhabitants pay homage to the God Pak Tai, Ruler of the North, placate the ghosts, and give thanks for surviving a plague over a hundred years ago. Extra ferry services are laid on for this event and some special tours are operated.

Tin Hau's Birthday. The main celebrations of the Empress of Heaven are held at a temple in Joss House Bay. Tin Hau is the patron saint of the fisherfolk, who come to ask her blessings for the coming year. Boats bedecked with silk banners fill the bay, and more than 20,000 people take part in the festival each year. Special ferry services are laid on for this colourful event.

May

Birthday of Tam Kung. Tam Kung is a local deity worshipped by the fisherfolk at a temple dedicated to him in Shau Kei Wan, Hong Kong Island. He is believed to be able to cure illness and subdue the elements. Celebrations go on throughout the day, and there is a magnificent dragon dance.

May/June

Dragon Boat Festival. This festival is celebrated throughout China to commemorate the 4th-century scholar/patriot Chu Yuan, who drowned himself as a protest against government

The Dragon Boat Festival is now a hugely enjoyable event, despite commemorating a tragic death

corruption. Boats went out in search of him and dumplings were thrown into the water to prevent fish from devouring his body.

The long, narrow dragon boats can be 100ft (30m) long and manned by up to 50 or so rowers, and a drummer dictates the speed. Team competition is fierce; races are held in various parts of the territory. This festival has become the occasion for an annual international dragon race event.

August/September
Hungry Ghosts Festival. The Chinese believe that this is the time of year when ghosts are released from Hell to roam the world and must, therefore, be placated with offerings of food, wine, paper money and incense. During the festival it is a common sight to see Hong Kong families burning prayers and money by the roadside and tables formally arranged with offerings for the ghosts.

September/October
Mid Autumn Festival. Weeks before this festival, coloured lanterns in all shapes and sizes appear in shops, making a delightful spectacle. On the evening of the mid-autumn full moon families take these lanterns with them to hill tops—usually Hong Kong Island's Victoria Peak—or beaches and parks, where they sit and watch the moon and feast on special moon cakes. This moon-watching tradition began in the Tang dynasty (518–907) but moon cakes—made of sesame seeds, ground lotus, dates and bean paste—are said to have appeared in the 14th century when messages calling for a revolt against the Mongols were put inside and smuggled to loyalists.

October

Chung Yeung. In the 3rd century BC, a scholar named Huan Ching was told that, in order to avoid major calamity on the ninth day of the ninth moon, he should take his entire family to a high place and spend the day drinking chrysanthemum wine. This he did, and on returning home all his livestock were dead, whereupon he immediately gave thanks. This custom has continued through the ages and has been combined with an autumn visit to family grave sites to make sacrifices of food, which are then picnicked upon.

CHILDREN

For younger members of the family, trips to Ocean Park (see **Southern District**, page 35) and the Space Museum (see **Kowloon** (Tsim Sha Tsui, page 41) are recommended. Otherwise there are very few facilities specifically geared towards children; but come during one of the many festivals (see **Special Events**) and they are sure to be entranced.

Even if Hong Kong is not the best-equipped place for children, its own unique charm can work wonders

TIGHT BUDGET

Hong Kong is not the easiest place to stay on a tight budget. The air fare alone can be all too hefty—but it is worth shopping around among reputable travel agents for discount fares such as APEX (Advance Purchase Excursion), which—be warned—can have several restrictions and conditions.
A few other tips might be worth keeping in mind. Trams are a cheap and often pleasant way of getting around, though slow. The fares are very reasonable for children. Hong Kong's public transport is not generally too costly (see **Domestic Travel**, in the **Directory** section). There is plenty of walking scope in Hong Kong, too: the HKTA (see **Tourist Advice**, page 123) can provide details of walks on the Island and in Kowloon.
Hostels and guesthouses are a good idea for an economical stay—see **Accommodation**, above. The Hong Kong Youth Hostel Association, Room 1408, Block A, Watson's Estate, North Point, Hong Kong (tel. 5706222) can give advice on hostels.
For bargain shopping, factory outlets have goods at wholesale prices, and the HKTA has a free list of member outlets.
Eating out is not cheap—even at the street food stalls—but a bowlful of noodles, meat, vegetables and beancurd can provide a filling meal at a reasonable cost. One cheap place to eat is the Poor Man's Nightclub – see **Food and Drink**, above. Drinks are sold at half price in Hong Kong during Happy Hour (17.00 to 21.00).

SPORTING ACTIVITIES

In spite of its small size, Hong Kong has many sporting activities to pursue for both the tourist and resident. Without a doubt, horseracing is the overriding passion during the mid-September till early June racing season. There are two race courses, one at Happy Valley on Hong Kong Island, and a super-modern complex at Sha Tin in the New Territories. Bets totalling more than HK$24 billion are placed annually. A convenient way to attend a race meeting is to join the Hong Kong Tourist Association's HK$250 'Come Horseracing' tour.
Taking to the sea is a natural form of escape and in the smart marinas, boating and yachting clubs, high powered sea cruisers bob alongside junks and sailing boats. The Hong Kong–Manila Yacht Race is held every Easter, while weekend races are held all the year round. Pleasure junks can be chartered by the day or half day; for information call the HKTA (tel. 7225555). Other water sports which are open to visitors include water skiing, diving, and wind surfing. The Royal Hong Kong Golf Club sponsors the annual international Hong Kong Open Golf Championship at its course at Fanling, in the New Territories. Visitors may play on weekdays only at Fanling (tel. 6701211) or at the 9-hole course at Deep Water Bay, Hong Kong Island (tel. 8127070). Golfing and other sporting facilities—tennis, squash, badminton, swimming— are open to visitors at the Clearwater Bay Golf and

Sports of all kinds are readily available to tourists and locals

Country Club at Sai Kung—the HKTA runs tours on Tuesdays and Fridays. See **Tourist Advice**, page 123.

Chinese martial arts are very much the vogue, and various schools of *kung fu* are taught under the guidance of highly respected masters. For information about *kung fu*, contact the Hong Kong Chinese Martial Arts Association (tel. 3944803).

In spite of the overcrowding in much of Hong Kong and the New Territories, it is possible to escape for long and delightful walks in the territory's hillsides and valleys. There are now 21 designated country parks accessible by public transport. The routes are clearly signposted and well laid out with picnic and barbecue areas and nature trails. Detailed maps are on sale at the Government Publications Centre, General Post Office Building, Central, Hong Kong (just by the Star Ferry concourse).

Hong Kong's main beaches are supervised by lifeguards and have changing rooms and rafts as well as barbecue areas. They are packed during summer weekends but not after the mid-autumn festival in September. There are some very pleasant beaches, but pollution has affected some of them, and the tides bring in plastic bags and debris, which are a curse for everyone.

DIRECTORY

Arriving

United Kingdom citizens do not require an entry visa. For short-term trips most visitors only need a passport.

The Hong Kong Hotels Association has a counter in the arrival hall and can arrange accommodation.

Hotel buses, metered taxis and airport bus services are available at the airport.

There are three regular airport bus routes: No A1 services hotels in the Tsim Sha Tsui area of downtown Kowloon. The fare is HK$6. Bus No A2 crosses the harbour and services hotels in the Central District of Hong Kong Island and the Macau Terminus. The fare for this route is HK$8. The fare for Bus A3, which services hotels in the Causeway Bay area of Hong Kong Island is also HK$8. Passengers place the fare in a collection box as they enter the bus and no change is given. These bus services operate between 08.00 and 22.30hrs.

Taxis charge a surcharge of HK$20 if they make trips through the cross-harbour tunnel. There is also an extra charge of HK$2 per piece of luggage. Taxi drivers are usually honest but should you have a problem contact the Royal Hong Kong Police's taxi hotline (tel. 5277177).

An airport departure tax of HK$100 is levied.

Car Breakdown

The **Hong Kong Automobile Association**, Houston Centre, Tsim Sha Tsui East, Kowloon (tel. 7395273) has an emergency breakdown service (tel. 3322617) which is available to all international AIT members. Non-AIT members should contact the nearest garage in case of a breakdown or telephone Da Chong Hong Motor Service, who have 24-hour centres in Kowloon (tel. 7546222), Hong Kong (tel. 5632222), Tsuen Wan (tel. 4993171) and Yuen Long (tel. 4790111).

Car Hire

The basic requirements for renting a car can vary from agency to agency but normally the driver must be at least 25 years of age, and have had a valid driving licence for a minimum of two years. Some companies will only accept credit cards in payment; it is best to check. Both self-drive cars and chauffeur-driven limousines can be hired.

Avis Rent a Car Systems Inc, 85 Leighton Rd, Hong Kong (tel. 8906988)

Dollar Rent a Car, Room 1204–6 Tun Ming Building, 40 Des Voeux Rd Central, Hong Kong (tel. 8452859)

Customs Regulations

The duty-free allowances are: 1 quart of alcohol, 200 cigarettes (50 cigars or 9 ounces (250g) of tobacco) and a small quantity of perfume. Firearms and weapons must be declared and will be kept by Customs until the visitor's departure.

Domestic Travel

Hong Kong's transport system is varied, efficient and cheap—it needs to be, to accommodate the pressing needs of its expanding population and mushrooming development of modern towns.

The picturesque traditional form of transport—the rickshaw—has died out and exists only as a tourist attraction. There are now no more than a dozen registered rickshaw men, who congregate at the Star Ferry Concourse. They will run you half-heartedly around the block or pose for photographs, demanding exorbitant fees which can be bargained down by the more determined customers to about HK$10–20 for a photo and HK$50–100 for a ride.

Buses The double-decker buses operated by the motorbus companies are, of necessity, functional—which means they are frequently overcrowded and bumpy—but services are frequent. Details of the bus routes are available from the Hong Kong Tourist Association. The bus fare—ranging from HK$1.20 upwards—is displayed inside the bus above the coin box beside the driver. No change or tickets are given, so it is advisable to have plenty of coins if you are intending to use the buses often.

Minibuses The cream and red 14-seater minibuses are a fast and cheap way to get around, but difficult for visitors to learn to use. The destination is displayed on the front of the vehicle in dominating Chinese characters, which makes the English underneath hard to see. They will stop—traffic regulations permitting—wherever you want. To hail one, just hold out your hand. To get off, just call out to the driver and pay him as you get off.

Maxicabs These green and white cabs have numbers and operate on set routes. You pay as you enter and no change is given. A particularly useful Maxicab service operates from the Kowloon Star Ferry concourse to the shopping and hotel areas of Tsim Sha Tsui East, Kowloon.

Taxis Taxis are still relatively cheap and are used almost as a form of public transport rather than a luxury. They can usually be hailed in the street, though in the busy business sections they are restricted by yellow lines as to where they may pick up passengers. Hotels and taxi ranks are the easiest place to find one and the most orderly. Drivers usually understand some English but not always. A Kowloon driver will not necessarily be familiar with Hong Kong Island and vice versa. Drivers work for 12 hours at a stretch and change shifts around 16.00. Taxis are scarce then, as they are on race days. All taxis are metered and the flagfall for the red, urban taxis is HK$6.50 for the first mile (2km), with an 80 cents charge for each succeeding ⅙ of a mile (0.25km). Extra charges include HK$20 for the cross-harbour tunnel and HK$3.50 for the Aberdeen tunnel. There is also a small extra charge for baggage. Green and white taxis only operate in the New Territories. Their flagfall is HK$5.50 and 70 cents for each ⅙ of a mile (0.25km).

Should you encounter problems with a driver, take a note of the taxi number and phone the Police hotline (tel. 5277177).

Trams There is considerable affection for Hong Kong Island's 85-year-old tram system, but its survival is under debate. The double-decker trams rumble gently down between Shau Kei Wan at the eastern end of the Island to Kennedy Town in the west. The ride costs a mere 60 cents and must be the best sightseeing value in the world! It is a pleasant and unhurried way to view the city, especially on rainy days. (Trams bounds for Happy Valley—a branch line—

Rides in or pictures of rickshaws are now a costly tourist gimmick

will not go the full eastern
journey, so check the tram's
destination.)

Passengers hop on at the back
and alight at the front, dropping
the fare into the coin box as they
do so.

One of the musts in Hong Kong is
a ride on the **Peak Tram** which
recently celebrated 100 years of
service. This exciting eight-
minute funicular ride offers
superb vistas of Kowloon and the
harbour as it scales Victoria
Peak to a height of 1,300ft (397m).
It is used by commuters too, so
there are jerky stops along the
way, and long queues form at
weekends and public holidays.
Tickets cost HK$6 single or
HK$10 return; the service runs
from 07.00 to midnight. A free
bus service operates between
the Hong Kong Star Ferry and
the Peak Tram terminus on
Garden Road.

In the New Territories a new
Light Rail Transit (LRT) system
operates between Tsuen Wan
and Yuen Long.

Ferries Cross-harbour and inter-
island ferries are an integral part
of Hong Kong's transport system.
The **Star Ferry** is the most
famous. Its green and white
ferries have provided the cross-
harbour service between Tsim
Sha Tsui and Central since 1898,
and they are as much a part of
Hong Kong's romantic image as
any full-sailed Chinese fishing
junk. The eight-minute journey
costs HK$1 first class, and 60
cents second class (lower deck).
The Star Ferry operates
between 06.30 and 23.30 at very
frequent intervals.

Other cross-harbour Star Ferry
services operate between

*The well-known Star Ferry makes its
way from Central District to Kowloon
every few minutes*

Central and Hung Hom
(convenient for access to the
Kowloon–Canton Railway
Station) and Tsim Sha Tsui and
Wanchai.

Over 300,000 commuters daily
use the Hong Kong and Yau Ma
Tei Ferry Company's double and
triple-decker ferries which
serve the outlying islands and
outer harbour. Ferries to the

islands of Lantau, Cheung Chau, Lamma and Peng Chau take no more than an hour and the deluxe class is air-conditioned, and equipped with an open sun-deck.

The Outlying Districts Services Pier is on Hong Kong Island, just a short distance west of the Star Ferry. If you are thinking of making an island excursion it is best to do so during the week, as the weekend boats are packed with local young excursionists.

Trains The Kowloon–Canton Railway was opened in 1911 and was then the final leg of the London—trans-Siberia—Hong Kong rail journey. It now operates only as far as the Chinese border at Lowu. Fifteen years or so ago, weary travellers from China could enjoy a gin and tonic on the train. The Hong Kong section of the railway has since been electrified and the journey between the Hung Hom Station, Kowloon and Sheung Shui—the furthest point you can go unless you have a visa for

Cable cars provide a scenic form of transport over the headland of Ocean Park (see page 35)

China—takes half an hour. The trains run every 10 to 15 minutes. It is an interesting journey, revealing the rapid development of the new towns and scenic views of Tolo Harbour.

A single ordinary-class ticket as far as Sheung Shui costs only HK$6.40, and a first-class ticket HK$12 (half fare for children). Stored value tickets, which may be purchased at the stations, can also be used on the MTR. The trains are crushingly overcrowded on Sundays and holidays.

On race days, special trains operate to the Sha Tin Race Course.

Direct through-trains to Canton (Guangzhou) leave the Hung Hom Railway Station four times a day.

Underground (MTR) This is not a complicated system for the visitor to grasp and it is a quick and efficient way of getting about in air-conditioned comfort. It was opened in 1980, and the engineering problems faced in its construction were of gigantic proportions. It is used by over one million commuters each day. The cross-harbour line from Central services the outer areas of Kowloon and Tsuen Wan in the New Territories. A branch line serves eastern Kowloon as far as Kwun Tong. The 14-station Island line services the eastern corridor of Hong Kong.

Ticket machines issue electronic tickets, which must be fed into the turnstile and retained by the user, so that they can be fed into the exit turnstile. The fare structure ranges from HK$2.50 to HK$6.00. Stored value tickets are also available. A HK$20 special MTR Tourist Ticket can be purchased at Hong Kong Tourist Association centres (see **Tourist Advice**, page 123).

Smoking, eating and drinking is forbidden on the trains. There are no public toilets on stations

Cars Traffic in Hong Kong drives on the left hand side of the road and all vehicles are right-hand drive. Road signs are written in both English and Chinese. Drivers must, however, be prepared for heavy traffic congestion, especially in the cross-harbour tunnel, and at peak hours. Hong Kong's roads seem to be constantly dug up and this, too, causes traffic delays. Hong Kong drivers are none too considerate, either. Basically, Hong Kong is being

drowned in traffic, in spite of the government's attempts to restrict private motoring through steep registration and licensing fees. Parking can be a problem, though there are a number of multi-storey car parks which charge around HK$10 per hour. Metered on-street parking is common, between 08.00 and midnight on weekdays and 10.00 to 22.00 on Sundays. Parking is prohibited wherever there are no signs expressly authorising it. Many Hong Kong residents employ a chauffeur to save time and frustration. Local people like to show off their financial success with expensive cars, and Hong Kong has a high ratio of Rolls Royce and Mercedes Benz cars. Licence plates, too, have significance and 'lucky number' plates bring hot bidding at special government auctions by Chinese millionaires. The money goes to charity.

The Hong Kong AA sponsored the first China Drive for private motorists in 1988 to Guangdong Province, to celebrate its 70th birthday. Over 150 cars took part.

Driving
See **Domestic Travel**

Electricity
Standard voltage in Hong Kong is 200–220v. All plugs are three-point but the size of the prongs varies.

Embassies and Consulates
Some 70 foreign consulates and high commissions are represented in Hong Kong. There are no embassies, as Hong Kong is still a colony. Apart from issuing visas the consulates

and commissions will deal with problems such as lost passports or legal questions. Many of them have active trade sections and can advise on business potential. A selected list follows:

Australia: 23rd/24th Floor, Harbour Centre, 25 Harbour Rd, Hong Kong (tel. 5731881)

British Trade Commission: 9th Floor, Bank of America Tower, 12 Harcourt Rd, Hong Kong (tel. 5230176)

Canada: 11th–14th Floors, One Exchange Square, 8 Connaught Place, Hong Kong (tel. 8104321)

New Zealand: 3414 Connaught Centre, Connaught Rd, Hong Kong (tel. 5255044)

USA: 26 Garden Rd, Hong Kong (tel. 5239011)

Emergency Telephone Numbers

In an emergency call the hotel doctor, or dial 999 or any of the following hospitals, which have 24-hour casualty wards:

Hong Kong Adventist Hospital, 40 Stubbs Rd, Hong Kong (tel. 5746211)

Queen Mary Hospital, Pokfulam Rd, Hong Kong (tel. 8192111)

Queen Elizabeth Hospital, Wylie Rd, Kowloon (tel. 7102111)

The St John Ambulance service: Hong Kong (tel. 5766555); Kowloon (tel. 7135555); and New Territories (tel. 4937543).

Guidebooks

Chinese Festivals, SCMP, Hong Kong, 1982

Hong Kong—A Complete Guide, Passport Books, 1989

Hong Kong—Insight Guides, APA Publications, 1988

Historical Hong Kong Walks,

At Wong Tai Sin Temple, joss sticks are burned, fortune sticks cast and food is offered to the gods

Hong Kong Island, The Guidebook Company, Hong Kong 1988

History of Hong Kong, G.B. Endacott, Oxford University Press, 1973

Myself a Mandarin, Austin Coates, Heinemann (Asia), 1975

Rural Architecture of Hong

Kong, HK Government Printer, 1981

Health Regulations
No vaccinations are necessary unless the visitor has been in a smallpox or cholera infected area within the preceding 14 days. In Hong Kong drinking water is safe to drink, especially in hotels, but many locals still prefer to boil their drinking water. In Chinese restaurants it is advisable to quench your thirst with hot Chinese tea rather than cold water.

Holidays
There are several public holidays, and the dates of most of them vary each year:
First weekday in January; Chinese New Year's Day and following two days; Good Friday and the day following; Easter Monday; Ching Ming Festival; the Saturday before Liberation Day; last Monday in August (Liberation Day); day following Chinese Mid Autumn Festival; Chung Yeung Festival; Christmas Day; Boxing Day.

Lost Property
Should visitors be unlucky enough to lose belongings, the Star Ferry Neighbourhood Police Centres at both terminals of the Star Ferry are very helpful (tel. Kowloon 7317278; Hong Kong 5243447). But any police station will handle lost property enquiries.

Money Matters
Hong Kong's banknotes come in HK$1,000, $500, $100, $50, $20 and $10 denominations. Coins are divided into the following denominations: $5, $2, $1, 50 cents, 20 cents, and 10 cents. Travellers' cheques and foreign currencies are freely exchanged. It is advisable to change your money at banks rather than at hotels or money changers, for the rate is more favourable.
Hong Kong's banking hours are from 09.30 to 16.00 to 16.30 on weekdays and on Saturday mornings until 12.30.
Credit cards are widely accepted.

Opening Times
Normal business hours are between 09.00 and 17.00 daily and on Saturdays from 09.00 to 13.00.
Banking hours are normally between 09.30 and 16.00 to 16.30 on weekdays, and until 12.30 on Saturdays.
Shops in Hong Kong usually open late and stay open late, depending on the district. Shops in Central District usually open between 10.00 and 18.00.

Personal Safety
Tourists can feel relaxed walking around and about Hong Kong, even late at night. Women on their own need not be particularly concerned. But one should beware of pickpockets, especially in crowds, and handbags should be kept tightly under the arm. Hong Kong residents are required to carry identity cards, so it is advisable for tourists to carry some identification.

Pharmacist
Chinese pharmacists abound, selling traditional herbs and remedies from ground toad cake to deer horn; many of them often stock a wide variety of Western medicines.
The main Western pharmacies include two companies which have numerous branches throughout the territory, but not all of them have dispensaries.
The largest is Watson's The Chemists, with shops in Melbourne Plaza, Hilton Hotel, Hutchison House, Pedder Street and Prince's Building in Central District; and in the Ocean and New World Centres in Kowloon. Manning Dispensary has branches in Repulse Bay, Causeway Bay and the Landmark in Central.

Places of Worship

Anglican:
St John's Cathedral, Garden Rd, Hong Kong (tel. 5234157)
St Andrew's, 133 Nathan Rd, Kowloon (tel. 3671478)

Roman Catholic:
St Joseph's, 7 Garden Rd, Hong Kong (tel. 5252629)
Rosary, 125 Chatham Rd, Kowloon (tel. 3685731)

Others:
Methodist, 271 Queen's Rd East, Hong Kong (tel. 5757817)
Union Church, 22A Kennedy Rd, Hong Kong (tel. 5237247)
Kowloon Union, 4 Jordan Rd, Kowloon (tel. 5693500)
Society of Friends (Quakers), New Hall, St John's Cathedral, Garden Rd, Hong Kong (tel. 8496780)
Jewish Ohel Leah Synagogue, 70 Robinson Rd, Hong Kong (tel. 5594821)
Bahai'i, Flat C–t, 11th Floor, Hankow Centre, Middle Rd, Kowloon (tel. 3676407)
First Church of Christ Scientist, 31 Macdonnell Rd, Hong Kong (tel. 5242701)

Police
Police officers wearing a red shoulder flash speak English. Emergency: tel. 999; Crime Hotline (including taxi complaints): tel. 5277177; Police Enquiry Office: tel. 5284284 Ext. 484.

Post Office
The General Post Office at 1 Connaught Place, Hong Kong Island is conveniently close to the Star Ferry concourse (tel.

5231071). The main Kowloon post office is situated on the Ground Floor, Hermes House, 10 Middle Road, Kowloon (tel. 3664111).
Open: Mondays to Saturdays from 08.00–18.00.

Aberdeen makes much of its living from fish; fishing boats and markets crowd the harbour

Telephones
Because subscribers pay flat monthly rentals, individual local calls are free and one can go into any shop or restaurant and use the telephone upon request. A phone call from a public phone box costs HK$1. The three area code prefixes for Kowloon, Hong Kong and the New Territories have recently been dropped.

Lantau is twice the size of Hong Kong Island but still has open spaces and peace and quiet

For information on new numbers, contact the HKTA.

Time
Hong Kong is 8 hours ahead of Greenwich Mean Time and 13 hours ahead of New York.

Tipping
Tipping is the norm and although bars, hotels and restaurants add a 10 per cent service charge, it is usual to leave a little extra—about 10 per cent—for waiters. Taxi drivers, wash-room attendants and porters will anticipate a small tip.

Toilets
Public toilets can be a problem; there aren't many of them, and they may leave much to be desired. People usually find it best to use the toilets in the big hotels, department stores or in the Star Ferry First Class entrance.

Tourist Advice

Hong Kong is a major tourist destination with more than four and a half million visitors a year. The government-subsidised Hong Kong Tourist Association (HKTA) is highly organised and offers a wide range of tourist literature, including factsheets on interesting places to visit, Chinese festivals, museums, walks, shopping and eating out. HKTA information centres are located at Kai Tai Airport Buffer Hall; the Star Ferry Concourse, Kowloon; and Shop 8, Jardine House, 1 Connaught Place, Central, Hong Kong.

Tours and Excursions

Tours are operated by private companies and by the HKTA. For information, contact the HKTA centres. Prices for the tours may change.

Hong Kong Island tours A four-hour morning or afternoon excursion around Hong Kong Island includes the beautiful southern side of the island, the fishing harbour of Aberdeen, the Peak and the Aw Boon Haw Gardens. Tour price: HK$80–90 (adult), HK$60–74 (child).

A seven-hour day trip, at the price of HK$130 (adult) and HK$90 (child) includes a city tour, Stanley Market, a museum visit and lunch on a floating restaurant in Aberdeen.

Trams can be hired privately for an evening through the HK Tramways Ltd, which also runs two *dim sum* tours daily on antique trams: one from 11.15 to 13.15 and another from 14.15 to 16.15. Tickets cost HK$120 for an adult and HK$80 for a child. Bookings are made at the Star Ferry piers (tel. 8918765).

To enjoy Hong Kong's harbour—the busiest in the world—at closer quarters, the Star Ferry Company offers daily one-hour harbour cruises: the Noonday Gun at 11.15; the Seafarers at 12.30; the Seabreezes at 14.15; the Afternoon Tea at 15.30; the Sundowner at 19.00 and the Harbour Lights at 21.15. Book at the Star Ferry piers on Kowloon side or Hong Kong side.

Other boat cruises in Victoria Harbour and Aberdeen fishing

harbour are operated by the Watertours of Hong Kong Ltd, and the Hong Kong and Yau Ma Tei Ferry Co. Cocktail and dinner cruises can be made aboard the Hong Kong Hilton Hotel's *Wah Fu* brigantine.

Kowloon & New Territories tours
There are twice daily five-hour tours of Kowloon, Tsuen Wan, Yuen Long, and the Chinese border lookout point at Lok Ma Chau. This is an opportunity to observe the village and town life of the Cantonese and to visit a walled village or a temple. Tour price: HK$80–90 (adult) and HK$45–70 (child).

The 'Land Between' tour emphasises the more traditional side of life in the New Territories —markets, fish breeding ponds and duck farms. The price of this full day tour is HK$220 (adult) and HK$170 (child); it operates Mondays to Fridays.

The Sung Dynasty Village tour visits a recreation of a Sung period (960–1279) town where traditional handicrafts, costumes and customs can be seen. The three-hour tours cost between HK$145 and HK$190 (adult) and HK$105–HK$128 (child).

Macau tours The old Portuguese colony of Macau by the Pearl River estuary, 37 miles (60km) from Hong Kong is reached by jet foils and hydrofoils which cover the distance in an hour. The cobbled streets date from the 16th century, when the Portuguese first established themselves here. The South European classical architecture of the old part of the city is delightful.

For information on tours contact the Macau Tourist Information Bureau, Shop 305 Shun Tak Centre, 200 Connaught Road, Central (tel. 5408180 or 5408198). Tours range between HK$350 and HK$700.

China tours One, two and three day tours across the border into Guangdong province to Shenzhen, Shekou and Zhongshan and to Guangzhou (Canton) give the visitor a fleeting introduction to the People's Republic of China. Tourist visas are required for China and CITS can arrange this (see **Travel Agencies**), but one must book several days in advance.

These tours are operated daily (except Sundays) by China Travel Service (HK) Ltd, whose branches are at 2/F, China Travel Building, 77 Queen's Road Central (tel. 5252284) and 1/F, Alpha House, 27–33 Nathan Road, Kowloon (tel. 7211331).

Travel Agencies
American Express International Inc (tel. 8448668)
Archer Travel Ltd (tel. 3691166)
China International Travel Service (tel. 8104282; 7215317)
HK Student Travel Ltd (tel. 3900421; 8107272)
Hong Thai Citizens Travel Service Ltd (tel. 5448833; 3778111)
Jardines Airways Division (tel. 3689255)
Sita World Travel (HK) Ltd (tel. 7232397)
Swire Travel Ltd (tel. 8448448)
Thomas Cook Travel Service (HK) Ltd (tel. 5454399)
Wallem Travel Ltd (tel. 8651777)

LANGUAGE

Hong Kong has two official languages: English and Chinese. English is spoken widely by the foreign community and in business circles, but not every Chinese will necessarily understand English, as many have come to live in Hong Kong from mainland China. The local Chinese community speaks Cantonese, the dialect spoken in the neighbouring Chinese province of Guangdong. Mandarin (Putonghua) is becoming widespread while other Chinese dialects—Shanghainese, Hakka, Chiu Chow—may also be heard. Tourists are advised to have the hotel receptionist write destinations down in Chinese. This will avoid a lot of confusion and frustration.

Bright lights and a lively nightlife in Wanchai

*A Chinese medicine shop.
Treatments can be thousands of
years old*

Glossary

can you speak English? *neih
    wuih mwuih gong ying
    mahn?*
**hello (only spoken on the
    telephone)** *wai!*
how are you? *néih hou ma?*
good morning *jóu sahn*
good night *jóu tau*
I'm sorry *deui mjyuh*
no *mhaih* or *mhou*
thank you (for a service) *mgòi*
thank you (for a gift) *dò jeh*
yes *haih* or *hou*
Hong Kong *Hèung Góng*
Kowloon *Gáu Lùhng*
The New Territories *Sàn Gaai*
The Peak *Sàn Déng*
where *bīn douh?*
how long does it take? *yiu géi
    nói?*
how much/how many? *géi dō?*

how much is it? *géi dō chín?*
dollar *mān*
one dollar *yāt mān*
ten dollars *sahp mān*
airport *fèi gèi chèuhng*
bus *bā sí*
Peak Tram *Laahm Chè*
tram *dihn chè*
taxi *dīk sí*
what time is it? *géi dím jūng?*
o'clock *dím jūng*
three o'clock *saàm dím jǔng*
minute *fàn*

Numerals

1	*yāt*	20	*yih sahp*
2	*yih*	30	*sàam sahp*
3	*sàam*	40	*sei sahp*
4	*sei*	50	*ńgh sahp*
5	*ńgh*	60	*luhk sahp*
6	*luhk*	70	*chát sahp*
7	*chát*	80	*baat sahp*
8	*baat*	90	*gáu sahp*
9	*gáu*	99	*gáu sahp gáu*
10	*sahp*	100	*yāt baak*
11	*sahp yāt*	1,000	*yāt chìhn*

Aberdeen 32–4, 61, 121
accommodation 93–7,
    109
air travel 109, 111
Amah's Rock 49–50
Ap Lei Chau 34
Aw Boon Haw Gardens
    26, 27–8

banks 119, 120
beaches 34, 35, 36, 59,
    110
birdlife 56, 61–2, 63–6,
    68, 70, 71, 72
Botanical and
    Zoological
    Gardens 20
budget tips 109
buses 111, 112

car hire 111
Castle Peak 46–8
Castle Peak Monastery
    46–7
Causeway Bay 26–8
Central District 13–23
Chater Gardens 20–1
Che Kung Temple 50
chemists 120
Cheung Chau 57–8
children's
    entertainment 108
Chinese University 50
Ching Chung Koon
    Temple 47–8
climate 101–2
clothing 102
clubs and bars 100
Colonial Cemetery 29
customs regulations 111
Deep Bay 65–6
Deep Water Bay 34
Dragon Pottery Kiln 48
driving 111, 117

Eastern District 26–31
embassies and
    consulates 117–18
emergencies 111, 118
Eu Yan Sang Chinese
    Medicine
    Company 16

Fanling 48
ferries 57, 114–15

festivals and events 30,
    98, 104–8
Flagstaff House
    Museum of Tea
    Ware 21
food and drink 73–86,
    109
Fung Ping Shan
    Museum 25
Government House 21
guidebooks 118–19

Ha Tsuen Village 54–5
Hakka Wai 48
Happy Valley 28–9
history of Hong Kong 6–
    9, 37, 45–6
Hong Kong & Shanghai
    Bank 20, 21
Hong Kong Island 12–
    36
    hotels 93–4
Hong Kong Museum of
    Art 21
Hong Kong Museum of
    History 41
Hong Kong University
    25
Hopewell Centre 31
hotels 93–7
Hung Shing Temple 30

Island House 53

Jamia Masjid Mosque
    41
Jardine's Bazaar 26

Kadoorie Experimental
    Farm 53
Kam Shan Country Park
    71–2
Kam Tin Village 54
Kennedy Town 25
Kowloon 37–44
    hotels 94-7
Kowloon–Canton
    Railway Museum
    53

Lai Chi Kok
    Amusement Park
    39
Lai Chi Kok District 37, 39

Lamma 58–9
Lantau 59–60, 122
Lau Fau Shan 54
Lei Cheung Uk Tomb
    and Museum 39
Lei Yue Mun Village 48
Lion Rock Country Park
    70–1
local etiquette 103

Mai Po Marshes Bird
    Sanctuary 56, 63–4
Man Mo Temple 18–19
mangroves 66–8
    maps
    Hong Kong 10–11
    Hong Kong Island
    18–19
    Kowloon 38
medical treatment 118
money 119
Mong Kok District 42–4
Museum of Chinese
    Historical Relics
    31

New Territories 45–56,
    101
    hotels 97
nightlife and
    entertainment
    98–100
Noonday Gun 26
North Point 29

Ocean Park 35
Old Supreme Court 22
outlying islands 57–60

Pao Sui Loong Galleries
    31
Peng Chau 60
Peninsula Hotel 41
Ping Shan Village 55
places of worship 120
Po Lin Monastery 59, 60
post offices 30–1, 120–1
public holidays 119

Quarry Bay 29

rail travel 115–16
Repulse Bay 34–5
restaurants 74, 76–85

INDEX/ACKNOWLEDGEMENTS

Sai Kung Country Park 69–70
Sai Kung Peninsula 48
St John's Cathedral 22
Sam Tung Uk Museum 42
San Tin Village 56
San Wai 48
Sha Tin 49–52
Sha Tin Race Course 51, 52
Shau Kei Wan 29–30
Sheung Yiu 48
shopping 15–17, 18, 19, 43, 87–92, 109
Southern District 32–6
Space Museum 41
sporting activities 28–9, 51, 109–10
Stanley 35–6
Statue Square 22
Sung Dynasty Village 37, 39

Tai O Village 59–60
Tai Po 53

Tai Po Kau Nature Reserve 68
Tao Fong Shan 50–1
taxis 111, 112
telephones 121–2
temples 17–19, 29–30, 31, 32–3, 35–6, 42, 44, 47–8, 50, 58, 60
Ten Thousand Buddhas Monastery 50, 51
time, local 122
Tin Hau Temple (Aberdeen) 32–3
Tin Hau Temple (Kowloon) 44
Tin Hau Temple (Stanley) 35–6
tipping 122
tourist information 123
tours 46, 123–4
trams 113–14
Tsang Tai Uk 51–2
Tsim Sha Tsui District 39–41
Tsuen Wan 42

Tung Chung Village 60

Underground (MTR) 117

vaccinations 119
Victoria Park 27
Victoria Peak 13, 22–3
voltage 117

Wanchai 30–1, 125
Wanchai Post Office 30–1
Western District 24–5
wildlife 56, 61–72
Wong Tai Sin District 42
Wong Tai Sin Temple 7, 42, 118
words and phrases 125–6

Yau Ma Tei District 42–4
Yim Tso Ha Egretry 72
Yuen Long 54–5

The Automobile Association would like to thank the following photographers and libraries for their assistance in the compilation of this book.

J ALLAN CASH PHOTOLIBRARY 7 Kowloon, 28 Happy Valley Race Course, 40 Tsim Sha Tsui, 42/3 Wong Tai Sin Temple, 49 Sha Tin, 50/1 Golden Buddha, 52 Race Course, 74/5 Floating restaurant, 86 Tea shop, 94/5 Victoria Hotel, 116 Cable cars, 118/9 Joss sticks, 125 Wanchai, 126 Medicine shop

NATURE PHOTOGRAPHERS LTD. 56 Pied kingfisher, (E A Janes) 62/3 Cattle egret (P R Sterry), 64 Great egret (M E Gore), 67 Mangrove swamp (E A Janes), 69 Chinese blue magpie (M E Gore), 70 Red-whiskered bulbul (M E Gore), 72 Skipper butterfly (S C Bisserot)

CHRISTINE OSBORNE PICTURES 9 Bridegroom, 16 Eggs, 24 Calligraphy, 39 Sung Dynasty Village, 57 Cheung Chau, 58 Beach, 76 Baked mud-crab, 83 Biscuits, 88/9 Local crafts

SPECTRUM COLOUR LIBRARY 15 Flower shop, 20 Hong Kong & Shanghai Bank, 31 At night, 34 Repulse Bay Temple, 60 Lantau Island, 73 Restaurant, 79 Larder, 84/5 Repulse Bay, 92 Hollywood Rd, 96 Regal Meridien, 98/9 Dancers, 104 Traditional costume, 105 Jugglers, 108 Children, 110 Tennis, 113 Rickshaw, 121 Fish market

ZEFA PICTURE LIBRARY Cover, Junk, 4/5 Skyline, 12/3 Waterfront, 23 From Victoria Peak, 25 Food seller, 26/7 Gardens, 32/3 Aberdeen harbour, 36 Stanley Village, 44 Sightseeing, 46/7 Castle Peak, 54/5 Rice fields, 80/1 Market, 91 Street market, 101 New Territories, 103 Fortune teller, 106/7 Dragon Boat Festival, 114/5 Ferry, 122/3 Lantau Island